The Essential Gorter – Volume 1

May

Herman Gorter

May

An epic poem about youth

After *Mei* by Herman Gorter, 1889, edition *Verzamelde werken* Deel 1 (eds. Jenne Clinge Doorenbos and Garmt Stuiveling), Amsterdam 1948.

ISBN 978-90-831336-45

May is Volume 1 of *The Essential Gorter* by Arimei Books. Read also Volume 2 : *Selected Poems*. Translated by Lloyd Haft.

Cover illustration & design : © 2020 Eva Polakovičová (evapola.com). Redacted by : Myrte Leffring, Vicky Francken and Anne Walter. Published by Arimei Books. www.ArimeiBooks.com - www.TheMayProject.org

Contents

Foreword

When I was choosing my angle to write this foreword for M. Kruijff's translation of Gorter's *May*, what crossed my mind was the American poet Robert Frost's famous one-liner definition of poetry: 'Poetry is what gets lost in translation.' As one who for decades taught Chinese poetry via translations, I can testify to the lamentably widespread truth of it.

Yet, I can also affirm that it is but a partial truth. Translations of poetry can themselves be poetry. I was more or less 'converted to' Chinese poetry by A. C. Graham's *Poems of the Late T'ang* (Penguin, 1965). Somehow the evocative elegance of Graham's phrasing in English, together with his commentaries which assured me that he really did know what the originals meant, gave me the feeling that I was missing nothing by not (at that time) being able to read the originals. Rather, I was gaining a new rich source of poetic enjoyment. Since then, as a scholar I have learned to read Chinese. But I have never lost a secret preference for poetry that has been brought within the easeful and matchlessly adequate milieu of my native language. To me the 'real' meaning of a text is in the words I would use in retelling it to myself.

After I arrived in Holland as a graduate student in 1968, I learned Dutch pretty quickly and by three years later was already trying my hand at translating poetry. I soon discovered Herman Gorter via his wildly experimental 'sensitivist' *Verses* (Verzen, 1890) – just about the most difficult thing with which to begin. I knew that Gorter was at least equally famous for a slightly earlier work, the epic

May (Mei, 1889). But *May* was written in regular meter and rhymed couplets, and for me at that time, this was reason enough not to read it. In the modern American poetry to which I was accustomed, it was considered slightly ridiculous to write in traditional forms – or, for that matter, to translate into them. One of my favourite poets, Robert Lowell, wrote in the introduction to his translations collected in *Imitations* (1958): 'Strict metrical translators still exist...but they are taxidermists, not poets...' So, to me for half a century Herman Gorter remained the poet of *Verses* but not of *May*.

Just a couple of months ago, in early 2021, I had an experience which confirmed me in the notion that poetry in a foreign language has perhaps the most depth for me when I can 'acquire' it in the language of my earliest childhood. I happened to come across M. Kruijff's new English rendering of *May*. Once I started reading it, I could hardly put it down – this 'despite' the fact that it is written in a slightly liberalised but still recognizable variant of Gorter's pentameter couplets. The English of Kruijff's version is certainly not everyday English whether British or American. Nor is it the flattened, cautiously academic English of so many translations. As I perceive it, it harks back to a somewhat earlier stage at which Dutch and English were still more obviously sister languages, both rooted in an older stratum of Germanic words, rhythms, and myths which was one of Gorter's own fountainheads while he wrote *May*. If the English sounds somewhat archaic, so does the original. For me, this strangely appropriate uncommon voice or tone makes the narration a delight to read.

Would Robert Frost have approved? I think so. Besides the wry quip on poetry and translation that I have quoted above, there is another statement by Frost, much less well known, that reads: 'Poetry is when an emotion has found its thought and the thought has found words.' It is clear from Kruijff's introduction and acknowledgments that his own process of translation began from a powerful emotion, proceeded through a years-long process of thought, and finally 'found words.' The words, time and time again, are as surprising as they are memorable. In other words, this is a poetic translation of a poetic original. It is with pleasure that I heartily recommend it.

Lloyd Haft
Oegstgeest, The Netherlands
October 2021

Introduction:
The melancholy in my May

The epic poem in front of you, *May*, first published in the Dutch language in 1889 as *Mei*, stands out as one of the poetic milestones in Dutch literature. This lyrically rich modern saga brings to life ponderings on many themes: nature and love, the perishable and the eternal, the physical versus the spiritual, youth and melancholy. It is the story of the short but wonder-filled, hopeful, intense, and finally tragic journey of the stunningly unspoiled girl, May: through the Dutch landscape of sea, dunes, and pastures, on an ambitious search within the spiritual world and finally into submission in the face of mundane city life.

It has been argued that there is a *May* for everyone. *May* can be viewed through many different lenses. Much has been written about its sparkling depiction of nature in spring, and about May's attempt and failure to unify the physical and the spiritual. And for good reason, as the first, second and third books of *May* cover these topics marvellously. It is difficult to capture in a single brief review the meaning and motivation behind a great work of art: it is hard to put a formal finger on the spontaneously inspired expression of an all-encompassing emotion – which *May* certainly is an example of. It is my hope that this translation will let you experience the same full spectrum of reflections as the original has done for many people in The Netherlands.

For me personally, *May* resonates with the sweet melancholy of my youth. I have always wanted to share that emotion with those around me but found that nearly impossible. In the end I realised that the best way for me to express it was by preparing and sharing a translation of *May*. Please allow me briefly to describe the melancholy in my *May*. It all starts, and every year again, with a new spring.

The spring as depicted in *May* is decidedly north-western European, with its wind-torn clouds in pale-blue skies over dark foamy waves and sandy beaches, their western flanks tinted pink and orange by the light of sunset in the salty air. Air thick with the scent of ozone. It is the spring that Monet immortalised in his painted impressions.

Yet the emotional association with spring is universal, and so is, more generally, the link between the months of the year and the cycle of life. It is so for many creatures of Nature. The primal response that this life story evokes in many supports the idea that this relationship between the seasons and our own lives is also deeply engraved in mankind.

In Roman times, March was the start of the cycle, the first month, the birth. Life grows, flourishes, explodes, levels, wanes, and finally withers and dies when the last month is reached. But life itself does not disappear – far from it. Every cycle plants the seeds for the next, and this seed magically refreshes and even increases life every new spring. Every new spring brings a new opportunity, a new hope, a new innocence, a new wonder. And in such boundless optimism the poem starts. A new sound.

Gorter chose to personify the month of May as the main character for his epic poem, quite possibly out of an already nostalgic love for the period of life it represents. Gorter was only 24 when he finished *May*, and as he looks back on his childhood and first love, as for many, the memory of this phase of life is heavy with a colourful melancholy, one that must be captured before it is lost. *May* chronicles childhood and early adolescence: the growing up from a small world of beauty in every detail within arm's reach not seen before, inside the endless sea of the unknown and looming loneliness; the first limitless love for another person – the greatest, unsurpassable love that seems to endow life with purpose and with the ambition to grasp for eternity; and, finally, the unavoidable confrontation with the limits of hope and innocence, the realisation of the unattainability of a perfect world. This is the moment when adolescence turns into grown-up life. Daily duties and city life take over. And that intensity of experience may never come back, may for ever remain the subject of nostalgia.

Melancholy is often simply defined as depression, but in my view, such a limited definition does not do justice to the depth and optimism that melancholy also embodies. Melancholy for me is an unbounded intensity of the senses, which due to the nature of most of reality, can sometimes be taken for depression. It borders on nostalgia perhaps: the realisation of the elusiveness of being, of the past that we struggle to remember, of beauty that we struggle to preserve, and of our feelings that can never be perceived by anyone outside our own body. Yes, in melancholy, emptiness and endlessness are experienced like deep holes and black voids with at best a few dim lights on the far horizon. But there is also beauty that comes with the brightest of colours. It jumps clawing at the eyes, engraving itself in them, it wants to be remembered and appreciated. It is magical, almost painful. Yet there is a draining sense of loneliness for not being able to share such an experience. This drives, I believe, the rich expressions of many melancholic artists. Indeed, this might be why melancholics can often only be artists. It might be why Gorter wrote his poem so elaborately and full of metaphors. *May* could well reflect a desperation to immortalise and share his feelings about this richest episode in his mental life.

If my personal experience can serve as one example, the realisation of my melancholy, the intensity of my experience of life, and the heaviness of it, came at age nine, when a friend of my father told us hunting stories one summer in the hilly fields of Denmark. We were camping, spending the evening with family and friends in a large tent, with only cloth to separate us from the sky. It may have rained that day, for I remember vividly the smell of soil and leaves, as my father's friend told us of the state of mind of the deer at night. For a deer, every night requires alertness if it is to survive to the next. There is no safety, and the cold or warmth, the wetness or the hungry drought inexorably comes as it comes. The lives of beasts collide, and in the dark, stories are played out between them that the morning doesn't remember. The hunter finds an antler, a dropping, deep footsteps in the mud, some hair on a twig. And suddenly from a silent bush bursts loudly a boar and the hunter becomes part of the story.

I thus learned the meaning of melancholy and to illustrate it, to test it, to nourish it, my father's friend recited to me many an episode from *May*, for he knew it largely by heart. I lived my life with an intensity of experience that sometimes scared me, often absorbed me. Whether I was photographing as many different kinds of mushrooms as I could find in the autumn forest of the Luxemburg Ardennes, climbing a tall, steep rock without my parents' consent, or drawing a poster to raise ecological awareness – father and son covered in oil – these were activities I was dedicated to much more than any external motive would justify: melancholy filled my life with necessity.

My episode of melancholic life ended about 10 years later. I never suspected it would actually end; it felt like an inseparable part of who I was. But when my father suddenly died of cancer when I was 18 years old, I, at the time deeply dedicated to my studies, was thrown into a search for myself. I wondered where my grief lives inside me. What is it that truly drives me? How come I felt so lonely? How do others look at me, how should I behave towards others? I think I lost my innocence, and with it somehow the melancholy; that part of me just evaporated and did not return.

This story is not unique. When adolescence ends, often melancholy wanes with it. Maybe this happened to Gorter as well. At first it feels like a relief, an easing of day-to-day experience in the face of duties, of work, of the pace of modern life. But then one starts to realise that what has replaced it is actually a kind of numbness. And you realise that people who have never known melancholy possibly have always been numb. It becomes a gentle torture to feel that one is missing out on the sensing of the nature of things that is somewhere out there, in the details. Indeed, in Nature. That flag moving erratically in the wind, undeterred and unaffected by the expectations of the world around it. That tile that does not lie flat, that always wobbles when you walk over it. And when you finally lift it, it bares a microcosmic world of tiny creatures, some of shapes and a manyness of legs you have never seen before, each living its tiny life in that tiny place. It becomes frustrating to find yourself unable to explain to yourself and others what exactly has been lost inside you.

You may want to recover some of that melancholy, search for it, try to revive it somehow. You start to revisit the same places, listen to the same songs, read the same books. You talk to the same people about the same things that submerged you into that absorbing state of mind before. Sometimes it works. But less and less.

Does the parting monologue of Balder, the young god that May so deeply falls in love with, give voice to this very same journey? When May finally finds him, he is searching for his soul, embittered by the loss of his eyesight. He can no longer truly experience all that is May: her elation or her youthful innocence. It is music, poetry, in which Balder still finds most of his former self. But he gets stuck in there, locked *within* himself. And May, heartbroken, disillusioned, cannot deal much better with her own loss. What remains for her is most people's reality: an all-absorbing effort to get by. But that is not her. And she withers.

It may only be back in nature, without the pressures of modern life, that one can remember that original spark. And it may pour into you a sense of gratitude and fulfilment that you have lived without for so long. In the forest, flowery dunescapes or in the mountains: that is where she thrived. You are back into the world of May.

Gorter's people, the Dutch, love the wind. They love to stand on the beach, even in autumn when it is cold, and let the wind blow through their hair, to get their feet back into that primal world, even for a moment. With each grain of sand carried by the wind through the hair, along the skin of the face or hands, some of the pressures of life are drained away. It is easy to appreciate the sun, a white blanket of snow and the silence of the ice. If one can appreciate even the wind, one can stand up to all seasons.

Thus I hope *May* can also impact your life if you let it.

There are more than 4380 lines in *May*. Each line, with its rigid rhyme and the pliable, reassuring regularity of the iambic pentameter, acts like one brush stroke in an Impressionist painting, putting you in a trance that plunges you into the idea that Gorter wants to share with you.

If you are young in mind, still blossoming and full of wonder, I hope this little book will invite you to entrust images and memories to the mind, and cherish the tinting of it by emotion and the filtering lens of retrieval. And if you once were so, but now are seeking the colour of your memories, these blessed abilities to create them, to soak in the light and dark of days gone by, to be that observant again, to open the mind once more to nature and its bare, beautiful, sometimes brutal reality, I believe that reading *May* could show the way there and lead you back to it.

To stand in the wind, the rain, the sun, the snow, whatever the season, and experience full appreciation and love of every single day. Of life.

M. Kruijff, March 2020

May

I

The spring is new and new the sound it brings[1]:
I want this song to be like whistling
I heard on summer days before night fell
In an old town along the calm canal –
Twas dark inside and through the silent road
A gloam had spread, but in the sky still glowed
A light, there shone a blank and golden flame
Over the gables in my window frame.
A boy was blowing like an organ pipe,
The tones were trembling in the air as ripe
As young red cherries, when the wind of spring
Rustles the shrub, its journey there begins.
He wandered across the bridges, by the border
Of water, slowly he went back and forth
Like a young bird that whistles unaware
Its bliss in calmness of the evening glare.
Many a weary man who ate his meal
At night, listened as to a tale, with zeal
And smiled, and while a hand that closed a pane
Still hesitated, the whistling remained.

And so I want this song to sound, but one
There is I wished my voice to shine upon
With more than laughing of her gentle eye...
Hail, hail, I feel her hands, the bow refined
Of her warm arm. A dome of blinded light
Takes my face mildly misting out of sight,
My voice burns in me like the yellow flame

Of gas in a glass cage, boles of oak the same
Burst out in twigs, their sprouting leaves unfold
Outside, outside: a new sound goes, behold:
A general, young, in blue and gold stands out,
Calls at the vaulted gate a herald loud.

Blue drifting sea, and water of the sun,
Refreshing flow from gold, I saw it run
On restless waves which let themselves be cleansed
And soothed by sunlight, ponds lay open whence
The waves like white and fiery rams were born
With foam in bunches, on their heads were horns.

But at its edge the seascape broke, it rifted
Again and yet again, above it drifted,
Like golden bees, clouds dangling in the blue,
A thousand puffy little mouths blew dew
And salt in rounded drops on edges and
On rims of red-lipped shells, which in the sand
Seem flowers, white and pale like cream and red
Like children's nails, while some were striped and lead-
Blue like the evening sky in wind and breeze.
Conches were murmuring their melody,
Placid, on whirring of the waves unberthed
More lucid rustling like in drier words
The moistened vowels, shells were rattling
In glistening water, glass and metal rings
And pebbles, and on wings of feather too
Brought bubbles full of music hitherto
A nudge of lighter wind. They farther there
Past dunes were entering Holland's garden where

The beautiful, the round and fullest sank,
Descended, burst, the sound of music rang,
More fine than voices, and from reverie
Each dune both far and near looked up to see.

A water-cradle far at sea – a bed
Where undulating sheets of foam were spread –
Is where a young Triton awoke, his face
Flowed over with a smile, this as the grace
Of water-hills around him caught his eyes
And overhead a tower-cloud in white.
His horn lay in his bare arm, gilded fair.
He blew in it, soft noises in the air
Like summer's rain rolled from the golden mouth.
Then laughing louder, he tumbled about,
Swam upwards through the waterfall, a gale
Of foam and snow, which floats in every vale
Between two water-mountains, see, he smiled
Nestling in whirly water, cradle-child
Only just washed by mother in her lap;
It floats in rounded droplets, ruby-wrapped,
Its arms are reaching, cooing goes aloft
From its small mouth; he drifted so, face soft
And round, 'tween lips the golden cup that cast
Fountains of golden tones, a milk-white vase
Alike he floated, wine was mixed within,
A fiery red blush pierced the porcelain.
Now seated in the water, wave on wave
He watches laughing as they swell and cave,
He bursts out more and stretches his fair arm,
And through the water goes a loud alarm.

The sea then became like a great stout man
Of ancient day and clothing, richer than
Exists now in this land: the velvet brown,
Silvery silk, black felt and peltry found
Far in Siberian Russia; and yellow
Copper burns tiny lights in plies and folds
Of pants, in buttons and embroidering
Of the wide robe, in breezes broadening.

Was such the sea? No, it would more compare
To city squares and streets during a fair,
The farmers and their wives, music and dance
In the taverns, and in the light garlands
Around the market, stalls of falderals.
Or when a king comes and light shines from all
The evening-windows, each and every roof
Flies its white flag. Such was the sea, flags too
Were placed on all facades, behind the window
Of waves fire-lights were shining in a row,
Together marched the nation. Mermen swam
Over with nymphs and elves, they rested then
On greenish slopes. Some Tritons though stood crumpled
Aside and old with beard, were holding trumpets
At their mouths, built long streets of sound and thence
Those went over the seascape's countenance.

Then it was quieter, a cloud of light
Started drifting nearby on the sea-sight,
Close to the clouds where there was a white crowd
Of young winds sitting and they laughed, first loud,
Then all things hushed. A yellow boat just had

Outcrawled the haze and, sheltered in it red,
Down by the linen sail, a child was seen...
Woe, woe to me, as my heart takes hold of me,
And my voice mutes now that this latest word
Was born… all things and places in the world
Enchant me in some way, and those who grasp
The same will go by waters, through young grass,
Feet fresh in meadow's dew each early day.
To them it's never hazy, but a May
Of children and a flow of flowers that
Surrounds their home, it's so for me too, yet
This child was purely, wholly loveliness;
So silently she stared, with happiness
Her eyes were shining in the shadow's light
Behind the sail, her face blushed in delight,
So pretty and *so* soft she was, rose leaf
Blown by the warm wind, as the forest breeze
Descends the creek beneath the hazel tree
And then arrives between the lower meads
Into the green and under skies of blue.
Could she, happy and full of wonder too,
Believe the water? Then safe laughs replaced
The wonderment, alternately her face
Turned to fountains of foam and the smooth crests
Of waves that waved in the white-blossomed beds
Of sea, or to the Wind that danced around
Like a young fellow on a grand fairground,
Or to a fish, that let its red fins rise
From the brisk water. All this was a prize
For a young girl's eyes. There far out, on his toes
A sea-god stood, his blowing lips enclosed

A golden horn. And all around from there
Sound broke as one from water and from air,
All new for one whom no one yet had bared
Such tunes; her head was fuller now, she closed
Her eyes in rest – the boat still floated most
Slowly ahead; unmoving shone the sun,
The wind walked with her and it walked along.

Who was she? Of twelve sisters she was one,
Hand in hand, alone, they stand on the sun,
Like children playing, standing close around.
In turn one breaks the ring and leaves that ground[11]
And leaves her friends behind in sadness, yet
Not many are their tears, a weeping met
By such a golden light one can't sustain.
So they are happy soon again, their pain
Will end – but *this* grief they've not felt before:
This latest void, with none there had been more
Laughter and for so long, she'd always be
The fairest, without envy, joy of each,
But now, now she was gone, the sisters' row
Bent over listening for where she'd go
As she was taken by the tide. Hazed sound
Of breaking foam and golden horns rose out
From mist to her. The children turned and stood
Together with their faces tearful, mute.
Those standing there present the fair blonde months,
The mother-moon gave birth to them at once
Heavy and naked in clear winter's night
Of stars, the sun though kept a watchful eye
Deep red and cold, he bore Aurora's look,

She wrapped them in a coloured cloth, he took
Them with him. See how blushing blonde they stand
In a close ring of fair blonde hair, one went:
The sweetest, blondest, yes, the little May.

No thing in the wide space is now as gay
As this earth: Cynthia[2] while on her seat
In her night-boat, exposes bright white teeth
In laughter and the twin stars halting near
Ask to themselves: will she be passing here?
The air is full of love and all rejoice
Where she has passed and where the gentle noise
Parts from her wings. With flowers left all about
Along her way, little angels call out
In unison her name, how full she was
With wonders. Lying in the thick of grass
That grows in meadows of the heavens, they
Are talking or just dream the day away.

One thing is sad and causes soft complaint
To forever circle earth, a mist so faint
And dim about that body: transiting
From being to not being of each thing,
Flowers and souls are floating to that realm,
A white and quiet place, where death shall dwell.
Because as always happens at year's end,
The migrant birds in clamour leave the land
And drop their voices from the firmament,
The children outside hear the ferment, bend
Their heads up, say: "The summer finally wanes,
The cold is coming" – in the clouds the chains

Of birds are gone – just like that all things pass.
But as I once was at the beach of sea
During the evening, yet my heart would be
Not satisfied but trembling, anxious too;
Like when across vermillion skies then flew
A bird, a black beast, one clear silhouette
That spread its tail and feathers – just like that
Arrives and leaves each thing, in loneliness
It's beautiful, the son of Restlessness,
Born in the twilight of its father's lap,
And unexpectedly it dies mid-step
Where death does strike it down – but while it lives
It represents the light: well, all I'd give
To see May's face all days she was alive.

Now past the banks she drifted, where a spray
Of red sand rushed down every wave, there stayed
People in groups, while in a cave of green
A mermaid and a water-god were seen.
May watched them and she laughed, heard briefly close
Resound soft laughter. From the water rose
A burst of clapping hands then, briefly too
Some babbling tongues, as sometimes women do.
But he watched sparkling and a red bloom went
Across her cheeks – when May stood up, her hand
Enclosed a silver box, one moment then
She stopped without a stir – a fold slid down
Her arm, crept slowly out of her white gown.
A hundred eyes then watched, all silencing,
No thing was heard except the shivering
That water made upon the foggy hills

And dampened laughter of those laughing still.
The silver flashed – and out there flew aloft
Two fluttering little butterflies, one soft
Yellow like ivory leaves from India,
The other patched, a shawl from Persia.

Changing their shine, the butterflies then danced
Across the surf, this is when May commenced
Her speech: "The long day finally finds its end,
See: in the cloudy west the sun descends
Already and it darkens, soon it's night,
I cannot stay. Now swim away. The light
Of the first star that touched my eyes just now,
Carries my father's robe and makes a bow,
While far beyond the east the moon awaits,
A rising light that diadem creates.
Therefore fare well. From here. And quietly,
I wish to bear my first night silently.
Look up, behold the moon, you see it's your
Friendly companion, go please, wait no more."

And just as ducks at night sleeping between
The reeds that grow in the canal, are seen
Sometimes to wake up suddenly, they quack
And dig up weed, one stands to stretch its back
Flapping its wings, it screeches high and thence;
Thus suddenly they left and quiescence
Turned into temporary violence.
But long persisted trumpets in wet sands,
The songs sung as a school of mermen swam
Off, lovers floated here, a young god went

Up to the crest high on a wave to see
If May stood where she stood – oh she could be
A little beacon white: that night the sea
Had one desire: to accompany
The waves that came to her. Many a prince
Declined to see his coral bedding since
They all stayed out under their capes where far
Away the water flushed beneath low stars.

Now left alone, she nearly filled with fear,
As she saw dark and sad waves come in tears,
Like women going round a dead drowned man
And one by one they recognise him then
They sway their arms in gesture wide and wild –
Just so in turn the crests collapsed, this while
They darkened more and more. Emptied by fright
Became her heart until from small clouds bright
A rain of rays came down, moon's golden sheen
Refreshed the water. Thus, I once have seen
A monk who stood by a dark and brimming cask,
Took out the plug, as he held glass and flask,
A spout of sparks poured cups as if the wine
Was full still with the sun of yellow Rhine.
Just so the Mother Moon stood in winds high
Turning the urn to pour the child her light.
Between the sea and clouds, light seemed to shine
Upon a cellar whence the wet of wine
Splashed clear over her foot. Round her full calf
While she was wading through the moonlight, laughed
Reflections of the moon in every drop;
And every time she saw it and she stopped.

The beach hosted a sand hill, like the fort
That children build, wet foam enters the doors
And moat when high tide rises, see them flee:
The bare and little feet, a growling sea.
Fishermen's children built it or maybe
The ocean-elves in summer sometimes seen
In morning, when the sun shines earliest
Its light on them, sufficing barely, just:
And from a distance then it may appear
That children leave in hurry without steer
The dunes, and naked, rosily they run,
Once sands turn white these boys and girls are gone.
The fort was built perhaps this way, where down
Against a wall she sat, with shells around,
Which moonlight turns to treasure troves of bright,
But only for so long, since when it dies
So does the glittering, what occupies
It then is not sweet sound: tormented cries
Replace the tunes of summer afternoons.
How horrified she was by the undoing
Of light by dark at sea and in the air,
Then milky shine once more when the moon fared
From the loose clouds into a blue-black lake
With sparkling stars, which withered in its wake,
Like little flowers that have grown in grass
Under a rose. The moon was generous,
Kept pouring falls of rays. The night unfurled
Before the heart calmed in that little girl.

And when she fell asleep, a mother leaves
Her child so when it dozes finally,

The moon-lamp muffled in her mother's hand,
Behind thin sheets of clouds it came and went,
A grey-brown skirted the low sky; a door
The hushing moon went through to leave, before
The last long rift that burnt went finally out.
She slept on the calm beach, lay safe and sound
Like any of the shells, while nothing moved,
Only the shallow water crept through grooves
Up to her ankles, with a flickering
In a light ripple, such as if a ring
Of rusted gold lay there, and water played
Around it with the jewel that it contained;
She lay in lavish sleep, so still and fair[11]
She blew calm puffs of breath into fresh air.

And there began then on the great wide stage
Of sea, like an old drama full of rage
In which the smell of blood, a murder's scream
Pervades the theatre – an empty scene:
A mad storm rages, at the high house falls
A chimney while the guardians on the walls
Can hear the sound of enemies in the fields.
The rain flushes and weeps, wind howls, there wields
A murderer his weapon, all can know
A corpse lies there as thunder rolls, the show
Is cruel: the moon now tears the stage with stripes.

The depths were moaning as once sailors griped
Who left this land for bounty and for loot,
They did return, with silver, piles of fruit
They took from the Antilles in vessels towed,

The fishermen saw how the sailors showed
The towers on the coast and when they passed
The quays, the men there saw the orange mass
Of lemons and apples, colours indeed
Of gold and silver too, they smelled the sweet
Incense that from the opened ports had swirled.
But when night came, with it the clouds unfurled,
The stout pillows that make night's lazy lair,
In which it rests so drowsily – from there
It saw the line break and the rich ship beached.
Through its dark lips the roughest laughter breached.
The moaning now seemed theirs: between the gold
Lay faces 'neath the water surface, old,
Both bleak and black as death, from their lips fleeted
Calls feeble like from men in desperate need,
Rocking in the water. That was horrible.
But May was deaf from sleep, impossible
For her to see a thing at all, she was
A nightly flower in lots of heavy grass:
She lay in lavish sleep, so still and fair
She blew calm puffs of breath into fresh air.

For long this awful howl climbed from the sea
Alone, it seemed as if the canopy
Of autumn forests wept with drops, or vile
A wind blows through a chimney, where a child
Is trying to sleep. It feels a weeping too
Inside itself, sleeps not, and deep into
The seascape went alone like this the sound,
Now high in darkness, where the wind had found
The rims of clouds and touched them anxiously,

Now low in drowsy waves where casually
Whales swam and drifted on their hulking hulls.
And then it sounded like the bittern's call
At midnight when it screams loud from the marsh
Such that the traveller in the bush and grass
That grows alongside the grey road, stands still
Below the shadow of the leaves; and filled
With wonder he moves on beneath moon-rays.

What is there in the twilight far away?
What touched the air so deeply? The coming home
Of all the fishermen? What sounds like foam
That leaves the sea? And is not what I heard
Like in a storm the scratching of a bird
That for a corpse washed-up beneath has come?
What is it, what disturbs the peace and calm
Of May who's opening her eyes and might
As well be a frozen, sickly girl in white?
Or are they maybe too her wondrous dreams
That make parade where sea and sand are seamed,
The white of waves is licking at their feet.
The eye of May comes glistening as they meet,
What do those dark men carry on their hands
Under monk's hood and cowl, hear them lament
The body on that bier; it's lying dead.
Still young is she; see how the blonde hair flat
And drooping down has April's flowered plaits.
Woe, woe, it is her sister, see our May
Longing to meet her, kiss her snow-white hand
That lies on silver shroud. It seems the sand
Though weighs her down, hear from her trembling lips

Poor sobs. Crows flutter as their crying rips
The sky to shreds, this while a muffled rush
Like round a dark house in a snowy gust,
Swirls round the feet which move already forth.
Oh child, be still and look at it no more.
For Death rides there, he's tall and pale a man,
He follows close behind. None other can
Give comfort, see, how he now passes there,
Still, still, be still, for those who died he cares.

Just as the sheep still late pass through the heath
In greenish evening light, are seen beneath
By those on moss-grown hills, while they move past
The heath edge to a road in dark high grass,
And round the bend – just so the dark gang went
And as she watched until the birds had spent
Their calls, they left the elongated sand.
Then fear sank from her face, her dreaming hand
Beside her, small and fair and lazily
It safely slept with her, but dreamless she
Herself lay there, her mind was blank, it seemed
Death took with him as he fled north her dreams.

Does someone know what is the fairest on
This earth, what prettiest comparison
He makes with all that gives him happiness?
Why does he love what in his nearness lives?
Why *one* wants riches, *one* a wife, his bare
Self one else, while they hardly are aware
That what they seek is more than just a word.
Does anybody know? Haven't you heard?

It's why the chick is seen to seek the hen,
The child its mother's breast, it's why I am
In fear of autumn, winter, the year's night –
It's why a young child does not love the sight
Of graceful stars but rather flame and flare
Of small white candles – with a candid stare
He lies awake in bed for long, his eyes
Will trace the wavy flickering of its light,
That flame burns long still in his sleeping mind.
It's why in music, songs, delight we find,
But marble and white colours seem so brute,
I love red roses, scents of shiny fruit,
The coat of peaches colourful and furry.
It's why a girl assures a man she'll burn
Inside his arms, her longing heart desires
The grand warm wedding hour. While she admires
Him for his love, what else could he have done?
It's fire and it's warmth, it is the sun.

The clouds now coloured, turned a light carmine,
From grizzled ponds welled up the dawn, and wine
Was clouding here and there between wave crests,
Like Bengal light, and though the waves collapsed
On it in foam, its laughter did not stop:
Thus in a water cup laughs the wine drop.
The sea became like Greek and ancient land
As found today, before in it would stand
Statues and temples of the empire tall;
Now columns lie mixed up with capital:
The stone worn down to lumps turned shadowy.
Carnations grow there now and honeybees

Suck nectar, still it makes one's heart heavy
When early sun just shines. – But soon it turned
Into a colour-dance that seemed to churn
A sconce of clouds, which still lay in the west.
A wind picked up, a flag in restless quest
Was flapping as a white swan flaps his wings,
His pinions launching trails of splatterings
Onto the water surface: feathers stirred,
Came loose – foam sprayed like that attire of birds.
And while the sun was gilding, mirror glass
In golden sculptures sailed at sea, there was
A play of colours and in every pit
More colours sprouted, different colours hid.
Here suds and bubbles, but there on the sand
Were colours of that playful wonderland
When shells are mixed together: violet,
The grey mother of pearl and amber, set
In little shells just as if from wet garnet.
A vapour rose from all of it, incarnate
Of all those lustres into one white blush,
Along the whole beach. But the sweetest rush
For eyes was May who placed in it her arms,
Awakening and rising on the palms
Of her flat hands, as frail shells were crackling
Underneath her – while on her delicate chin,
Still moist from sleep, a tilted sunray shot
Off the dune's edge, and made for trembling blood.
She looked past it, towards the sun to see,
Started to laugh, jumped quickly to her feet,
Then fixed her wrinkling dress such that the knee
Was bared – she paused then momentarily –

Whoever at the full canal could see,
Through summer heat and meadow, in blue reeds,
A forest nymph laughing like this, not far
Were heard the birds, the singing of a lark,
A roach emerged, a floating damselfly
In blue and she took flowers from the rye.
Such laughter I heard sometimes in the heath,
Late in the afternoon when a dark bee
Thundered its load home on determined wings.
The hills were darker now, though carrying
Still yellow-purple from the western rim;
Fresh satyr eyes with glitter watch a nymph,
She passes lowly wood, a shuffle and a shift
Rustles through withered leaves, I see his quiff
Go steep before the sky; then breaks the still
Soft chatter, cheerful laughs behind the hill.
She smiled the way a bird can sit for long,
A nightingale, caressing air with song,
With open beak and on a twig, in peace
Above a forest pond, the canopy's
Not letting night-light pass through well, noise swells
Beyond the thicket, but above all else
The black and tiny bird chirps quavering. –
Likewise, her laughing mouth let cloudlets spring.
She stood like this for long, then on she went,
Her red and little feet disturbed white sand,
In her fair mantle draped with golden hair,
Fast running she made gestures bold, with flair
Of children waving arms and hands, shrill yells
She uttered like the ringing of sledge bells.
There on the steepest dune, see where she stands,

In waving marram, round her face hair strands
In windy curls make whirls, a soaring fall
Of streaming gold behind as if the hall
Of heaven emptied over gilded steps,
And gold obscured the blue, applauding claps,
Clean linen waves in wind and yellow glows.
What a lonely sea, now that she landward goes.

And her magical journey now begins,
The moon thus floats into the sky, the wind
Is rising too – let all now see her here.
Because to those who have, the whole long year
Brings joy in plenty, and in winter night
They still will see her eyes. She skips so bright,
Her arms swing on the beat like a ship's spar
In waves. The wind is following not far,
And now she's walking through sun's golden spree,
In hot glaciers of sand, she walks the lee.

Between all dunes of which she climbed the peak,
The valleys welcomed her and they would seek
Her, pray for her to stay; there was a queue
Of flowers side-by-side yellow and blue,
Much like the people at a theatre.
All called her name, watered these beaks of theirs
The yellow harmony and narcissus,
Soft dangling purple-yellow chalices
Of happy pansies between moss and root,
Cold little snowdrops in the underwood.
To no avail; once seemed her journey's end
A still dune-pond, a pool for birds that spends

Wholly its summer day a mirror for
The yearlings that graze from the air before
They herd towards the stables, there afar
Where heavy beasts already lie, a star
Of evening burns; and when that evening comes,
The birds descend in it, the bee there hums
Along the hills, dunes fill with faint echoes
Of evening sea, straw bends and waves and goes.
And it was there she stood to sip a drink,
Lips in her hollow hand – the water winked
Its eyes just where the little droplet fell,
In light-green grass; tightly the water welled
Around her heel, while silence had returned
And very still, her eyes then had she turned
Beneath and saw herself. A happy fright
Surprised, caught her off guard, and in that trice
She did not think, was sweet with sentiments
Of friskiness, elation – cool still then
Lay there the well – she took a timid step
And saw herself ablush before a slab
Of mirrored blue, much like a ruby red
On royal robe. It's true, a sight like that
Is such a feast for eyes: with lips curled well
Towards the bowl she kneeled to kiss herself.
But as the four lips touched, her eyes received
Their own reflected shine, she was deceived,
For water wiped its ripples rude within
The cheeks of the delightful child, her chin
Was bobbing with the waves. She patiently
Then waited till the wrinkles waned to meet
Their end against the beds. A droplet chain

Dripped from her mouth and in this fertile rain
A little daisy hatched then from the ground,
A kiss of May. With flowers all around
She watched the little white crowns till the pool
Held still her image, and as if with full
Attention she read letters of her grace,
She moved her lips, until she raised her face,
Self-conscious, shy, if one was there whom she
Could tell. But just the sun was there to see.

Yet from the pond a little brook ran lone,
The water just a jewelish light, a stone,
A marble rock in sandy bed, lets go
Quicksilver lustre there where a thick growth
Of river grass is found. And on the banks
Are standing young with heavy leaves the plants,
Who are the listeners to the soft fanfare
The water makes. It jumps and falls from there
In black and babbles lower in the shade.
The ivy and the ferns listen in wait,
The higher trees not really, glistening
In sunshine and in wind, their evening
Is crazed with starlings' tweets. But late at night
The water's heard beneath the tree owl's flight.

She walked there like a butterfly in white,
Her legs through multi-coloured flecks of light,
Like mottled marble, a vibrating glare.
She then climbed down the waterfall to where
The brook gave mouth between two fields and brushed
Them both. A willow stands guard there robust,

Brute oxen come to drink the stream when eve
Falls red, there late and lazy fall its leaves
Novemberish, and lazier there shine
In unfamiliar months young summer signs.
At the narrowest grassy edge there lay
Between some alder and a hedge of may,
With reddish buds a flower basket stuffed
With vivid flowers and with lilac tufts
As garland, 't seemed a flower overdose,
But way inside in half the light, there rose
Yet one more buttercup. The weak sand sagged
Where May now put her foot, her ankles dragged
The crystal water through the brook, its trace
Quickly erased; as if the water face
Took pleasure in that little foot, it seemed
The leaves were playing spirals on the stream.

And barely back on land, there on that edge –
A child will look thus round the door to catch
A glimpse of promised cake – and she saw flowers,
Walked straight to there, and 'neath the hedge, she bowed
Head, made the blossoms rock, and jubilant
She flung the basket so it overturned.
Then scooped her hands with flowers and dew and danced
Through all the field; the clovers had no chance,
She clothed them all with decadence, just see
How round the dancer flowers whirled, a tree
Sprinkling its leaves heavy with rain, does not
Drop this much of its canopy – twas not
Unlike the rustling, coloured candy thrown
St. Nicholas eve, or when on Easter morn

The painted eggs are hidden in the grass.
She danced around, of benefit it was
To all the meadow and the brook as well,
For, as a fountain-spout will in its well
From column turn to tiny drops, no more,
Like that fell near her shoulder bloom in scores.
As she threw them, the air would spread them thin.
To jostling of a magician akin
With balls of satin making coloured bows –
So fell a lot of flowers in the flow;
It took them with it, stuck them to the bounds
Of the estates, and Holland soon was found
Alight with little flames. The pastures' whiff
Fills sails of ships, and rich blossoms adrift
On wind adorn the orchard trees for miles,
No burden to them, they'll just stay a while.

Then 'neath the hedge her tired self she laid,
A calf alike that slowly sinks its weight
Onto its feeble legs, chin fully in
Her hands. And then occurred to her this thing,
And long she thought how May's delightful work
Was now in silence happening. A church
Is dressed like this: the columns carrying
The arches, sculpted full with figurines.
The belfry houses workers who were aproned;
The floor is being laid, the window painted.
Out on the street it's hardly heard. – She thought:
"Should I now go, see whether I have brought
The bloom and blossom to the apple tree,
The old heat-wall bloodies the mulberry,

The vine embraces the old threshing barn.
Or shall I stay, make water-play, make fun
With butterflies that dance there in the portal
Of pastures. Shall I rather seek the sorts
Of elder wood from which I'll bore a flute,
Then blow its sound past hedge of thorn and root
Into adjacent land, calves cowering
Away. Or let's seek mallow flowers in
The field, and there's the hazel which can be
So soft, in alders' cosy company."
She thought this, but a butterfly then chose
While dancing right before her little nose,
Winking and blinking that the script of wings
Was difficult to read, its imprintings
Were runes that code a fancy mystery
That's known in India as rhymery
On creamish-coloured eastern tapestry.
She knew this well too, when with levity
She played her fingers, seeming butterflies
Themselves, to catch it in her hands, her eyes
Peeked carefully in the red cage, and weighed
The yellow captive with its pollen freight,
On fingers spread. While on her back she lay,
One knee over the other, without wait
Her lips would read it. Long then did she stare
At heaven, neither jubilant nor scared.

Until she turned around and let her cheek
Lower the coral off her arm, and squeeze
To oval what was pillar-round till then.
And when she gazed over her shadowed hand,

She saw two eyes, a woman's body lay
Upon the dew like her, was sprawled out straight,
In the next meadow, 'neath the shining sun.
Her voice was like her eye-light; it had begun
To sound and it was like a diamond:
"I've lain here since you have been smiling at
The flowers on your side, and yes lay I
Here even when grey ice was reason why
That waterfall choked nigh. In winter's night
I many times went up, stood guard there right
On that same dune when I heard distant calls –
They're mocking even during winter colds
And season's storm – the Triton brought them forth.
But when I was up there, I saw the north
Lit up by polar ice, still lucid blue
Like winter equinox, the cold passed through
Me shivering in tears; I then came down
Again and here I lay, my dreams surrounded
By spring and you – until the mist of dawn
That marches on the farmland, had withdrawn
And also birds flew earlier again.
I searched for flowers; at last they're in your hands."
She said so and held still, her comrade asked –
It was like birds that make an early pass
And swirl through town streets, then together go
And pick the ground to eat, the doors still closed,
And windows shut yet, nobody had stirred
But birds alone – and so that landscape turned
Now silent too with all its haulms, the creek
Nibbled its curbs no more, the willow tree
Kept still the noise of its white little leaves,

At its den, a brown dune-hare lay quietly –
"Can you hear well the mumbling of the sea,
A sound so dear to me, won't you agree
It hurts a little? See my sisters stand
High on the sun, they too to it attend,
They're serious a little: it always speaks
So lonely, sometimes more as if it weeps.
Yet on the sun I would so much adore
Still listening to its sound, it was the source
Of what we knew of happenings on earth.
One hears all sorts of things within its verse,
Because it knows both clouds and light of sun;
In this way I learned names from which I spun
Me wondrous things myself, I was so glad
When finally it was my turn. I've met
A thousand things whose name I now could say.
Till I came here and found your fair bouquets
And you. Who are you? Do you live alone,
Is this your water, have around it grown
These flowers as your children? And I thought
They've waited all for me to reach this spot."
She said thus, hushed, and when through foliage
And blossom underneath the hawthorn hedge
The breeze turned quiet, from the sunshine spoke –
A small old village bell alike, that woke
When summer noon chimed for the country folk –
That woman: "Pretty girl, your voice invokes
The cooing of a ringdove cock who woos
The female from a rusty oak. Suffused
You leave my ears, with flattering sounds; with zeal
I'd want to stay and listen to this peal,

Your mouth: with honey filled abundantly,
Sweetness of flowers, taste of mead for bees,
To go to that small palace, scrutinise
That dimple in your chest, a paradise
Of blood and shadow playing there, Zephyr[3],
Who blows into the meadow, must breathe here.
But rather I should turn away from you,
Avoid your eyes while I will tell you who
I am. Look at the fizzing of that puff
Of cloud as it evaporates above,
The sun comes home, midway on its blue path
And laughs behind its frame. And hear the bath
A sparrow takes rubbing its feathers in
The stream, a motley calf is splattering
In a creek, from the wood a cuckoo calls.
How quiet all; the cloak of leaves that folds
And weaves around the trees hangs idle, still,
I'll tell of me now, please do listen well:
I in the middle of this land was born.
There is a pasture wide, where you'd adore
A lark that's singing, flying to the blue,
The grazing cows that leak the fairest dew
And seem like boats afloat on stream. White wives
Are chased by wilful wind into the skies
Under the rising moon, a fog roams far
Still on the fields, fading the evening star.
Under the sun lie the canals, both high
Heavens and clover-pasture open wide,
To no avail a bird will seek a tree
Between; and you can hear the many screams
Of ducks, because a creek makes there its cruise.

On summer mornings farmers' wives there ooze
The cream out of the udders, vivid glittering
Of copper handles, milky buckets clattering,
A metal headpiece glimmers golden shine.
Right next to it the sea, no yellow line
Of sand lies there, while spike-rush and grass flowers
Fill up the meadow frame. A lonely Pharos,
This wooden balefire, from its top a light
Burns bravely, as it rises in the night
From water waltzing round it, when a ship
Sails dark into the river and in skip
Small elves turn white in foam at its high bow.
There lived my mother, and she was endowed
Abundantly with comfort giving birth
To me. For reed sheaves bending down gave word
To th'canal which to th'sea which to th'lagoon
Of light, where after noon the cloud-platoon
Sails solemnly. Thus heard the news a fish
Then seabird too; the cattail thicket splished
And splashed that day 'neath feathered waiving white,
Seagulls, grey heron turning for the night
To its tree nest. I saw during its trips
Its wings beat from between the scrub and twigs,
My nursery. Still I remember then.
My mother was a stream-lady and when
Hung prancing brightly the moon's disc, I saw
How she came up to me, a lady tall,
And closed my eyes with her sweet hand's soft strokes.
As soft as willow blossom and as smoke,
As if the roses had poured out their morning
Drink, all the night there sounded one performing

The zither on the sea, it may have been
My father's play, for him I've never seen.
There I grew up, lived like a little lamb
That's gambolling beside its mother, and
She held me close to her, a woolly sheep,
I heard her heartbeat till I fell asleep,
While out from my warm residence I looked
To the horizon, where it seems a brook
During the night streams on the bottom seam
Of heaven, dark and blue; and like a dream
It seems the high reed rocks to lullabies,
Under rare stars that burn like fireflies.
When autumn came though and the stork flew thither,
The grass still green and fresh now soon would wither,
When water early darkened, air grew cold,
Then also we went where in the remote,
Blue herons nested high in canopy.
The silent timber-fire was in the lead,
And ruddy leaves cascaded down in moss,
The thicket creaked and resin-pearls would toss
And free themselves, while wind flared up the flames.
We walked there and between the boles in rain,
Soon saw white women wandering here and there
Like us. And when the freeze of autumn air
Makes water shiver in its stream, begins
The great migration towards summer winds
For those who love the summer sun. They go
At night, who all stood guard at pond and flow
Throughout the summertime. They gather and
With satyrs and with elves on heather land,
Amidst them also their king Oberon.

Titania[4] too is there and holds her crown
Of spider-weblet drops where sparks appear
In moonlight; in her eyes, those jewels, a tear.
She speaks farewell to all the nymphs, don't stray
And do return with a new water-play,
Yes, all of us have felt for you such love.
She kissed me then, and oft when on my path
Through heath I turned my head she sat with some
Sad gnomes, and on a hill they beat a drum
With wistful minds and played the sombre lute;
We heard the motley tunes of panpipe flute
And ringing tambourines upon our road,
Embezzled barrels full of wine were stowed
On satyrs' back, and nymphs brought gilded plates
So full of bunches blue that spills of grape
Syrup were soaked up by their fluffy furs.
My mother called me, when the woodland stirs
Were pounding through the mountains, a crevasse
Of stones let wind and shrivelled foliage pass,
The hailstones pained the naked chest and grit
Would bruise the feet. Until we came where sits
In his high home the southern sun, a host
Hospitable, where from the ceiling posts
Falls turquoise tapestry, against the walls
Root marble columns; rosy annuals
Swing slowly in festoons from flower lands,
At day he fills his home with golden glance,
A draught he makes on blue lakes and a sway
Of pines and poplar trees where mountains lay.
My dwelling was a pink and yellow weed,
A marble vase with ears and swelling hid

A rose stalk and myself, a path went down
With golden sand, it ran from there to town.
And dark-skinned children came to visit here
With purple cloth around the head, and ears
With golden rings, young mothers with full bust,
A barefoot monk, a beggar with a crust
Of bread, an ass with red caparison,
Bagpipe and multicoloured garrison.
The air was hot in the rose bush, my gaze
Touched dreamily these people so ablaze."
She thus said, May then looked with her just like
A child who sees high in the wind a kite
Of coloured paper. Just the kind of talk
For a warm day and for the women folk.
Twas as if still the words she said before
Were on her mind when she spoke fresh: "The north
We turned to once again when came young leaves
On the old trees and simultaneously
With us the migrant birds, canary, finch
Who lives here also: you can hear it sing."
She spoke but hear herself she barely could,
She took her hands then from her lap and stood
Up like a white beast ruminating on
The field. She gazed, though, concentrating on
The far and silent canopy in which
Gleamed white a grange or spire, and said this:
"For what I still must tell you, no meadow
Or light is relevant: the May-month's glow
Of afternoon would make the tears go dry
That would be weeping out of your kind eyes,
That almost weep, as I of weeping speak.

You'll live still long, perhaps will find my creek
Again, one day when a white winter-mist
Conceals the woods once more and you have missed
A path. Along the water take a walk,
You'll hear it babble well within the fog
And find me in a haze; I'll make you pale
As water of the rill beneath the veil."

The air and sunlight then turned dull and glum,
When she departed, nothing but a drum
Was heard, of a tall horse in grass now frail,
That scared trotted around with loosened tail.
Through boles and dead brown leaves of previous year
She climbed into the dunes, then disappeared.

In all things hides fine essentiality
Of other things. Thus one's humanity
Will be like a piano: dead, but stringed.
Sometimes one string and then the other rings
In tune with sounds outside, then synchronous.
That makes even a poor and still man rich –
And feelings stand with him asleep in rows,
In turn they wake up as from boy he grows
Into old man. – Ah, many themselves dreamt
To death, until their life expired with him
And all was done – like in a fairy tale,
Enchanted palace locked behind a veil
Of ivy, hen and chicks; indoors, serenity,
Pages and damsels, guards were sent to sleep.
But when a prince arrives and breaks the spell,
The gate awakens, gives way wide and well,

Then chambers lie exposed under sun's rays,
And people wandering about, once raised.
Such is the soul of man, where each thing can
Call up each thing out of the muffled ban
Of sleep, so let it chime just like a bell
In its front hall, or at the water well
An echo from its deep and distant woods.
Music lures from the soul more music loose,
That treads in wondrous shapes out from soul's gate
And seeks this sound that so much fascinates.

And thus while to this child the tale was told,
Were entering images the mirror hall
Deep in her soul. She seemed herself to walk
Among them, whimpering and pale as chalk.
It turned into enchantment of distress,
She for the first time felt how sweet it is,
That loss of joy, how warm the source of tears
Can overflow the heart; then disappears
The sun, the soul is hosting play of fog,
Soft moonlight too and slowly turning cogs
Of airy waves in seas of suffering.
She felt the gentle swell of sorrowing
And closed the eyes, so it would not break up
For sunlight as a flower bud for drops
Of dew. – But as a youth or adult fares
Their hurt is as the child a mother bears
In pain, that then still dies – likewise, her grief
Retreated. And it looked like smoke that leaves
The chimney and that makes some silhouettes,
Till where the wind disrupts their delicate

Envelopment.

                        And Zephyr still remained
In shrubbery and she walked there. He trained
His bass voice but restrained when he discerned
Her shape, said smiling, offering his hand:
"Do not stay here, my voice is still too crude
For ears of that mother of pearl. For you
I'll sing a song right when my throat will feel
More thawed, now I will play this glockenspiel
Of yellow blossom." Yes, he so did say
And shook a little tree, then fell on May
The golden rains. He added to the play,
Attentive, at the stem, a poppy-rose,
That bent till then in wind with clover close.
It turned a lovely yellow-red bouquet,
Fine needlegrass he added and then gave
Her some – "I have no time for garlands now,
It's time to sing." And wide he gaped his mouth
And sang – and laughing loudly there she stayed.
Then he looked angry. Then she went away.

That was past noon. And from the woods went out
A sun's gold softly breathing steam and loud
The songbirds sang and they flew underneath
The tree crowns; from a plank-bridge she could see
Them beat their wings over the crystal stream:
The blue jays on the quay of green, it seemed
The ice of becks splashed thereagainst, the froth
Remained like coloured dripstone, and in rough
Mood white-black magpies fighting out the day,

And gliding down an oak the flickers swayed,
The smaller tree folk: robin, great tit and
A yellow thrush, and never tacit went
The blackbird. Everything sat very still and
Quiet as she walked on and eyes watched, brilliant
From branches where two doves rocked in headdress,
A blade of hay descended, came to rest.
She seemed a white bust as onto a lane
She went below where twilight never wanes.
In morning dim there melts a coolish damp
From dew, in afternoon the yellow lamp
Of light burns hazily. And where the lane
Hit croplands of a broadly stretched terrain
Adjoining lazily a hill, she sat.
The sky was clouded like a lake that's set
In rocks. The clouds swelled upwards far away
And eastbound where horizon's archway lay
And bent around the land. A duller light
Of bonfire, red like Alps at evening tide
Glowed on those snowy mountains. Motionless
She sat, a little bird in quietness
Sat close to her a while in a birch tree,
Abruptly started singing – she could see
It huff. It carolled in the air aloud;
Around the bird a golden brume drew out
From timberland.

                And it was five o'clock,
She saw in black a ploughman like a log
In soil, worn by his day of work, and bent
Over his spade. He watched in thought a span

Of mares that through the furrow someone drove,
At the end the bulky colter turned; a drove
Of deep-black farmland birds flew from the crops.
He wiped away with a red cloth a drop
Of sweat, he mumbled, and no longer stalled.
Gold flakes were snowing on his overall.

Deep from the forest came some pleasant noises,
A tripping on the air of wheels and voices.
There was a road paved with fresh yellow grit,
A logman finds his way to town on it;
After the noises one could see process
At first the children clothed in bright red dress;
Between them wreaths of flowery design.
And bigger girls in white with hands entwined,
Who walked under the fir trees so to stay
In grass. Back on the road the farmers' wains,
That spun up yellow dust under the roll
Of wheels. It was a wedding; like a doll,
With lace and jewels sat beautiful the bride
Above the surging dust and flowers high.
The horses went in step with ringing sounds
Of harness bells, the ploughman tried to count
Them all and waved his hat: the chatter veered
High up then, on that yellow street, to cheers.
And when they were emerging from the green
A quiet glaring of the sun was seen
In wrung hard wood of carvings on the cars
And on the wheels in copper hubs and bars.
So the parade slid past in one close string,
The racket went, and man turned figurine.

Just flower tints gleamed visibly, the white
The girls wore, and of horses the steel bit.

And there between the slopes lay in the light
A foursquare field with flowers set upright,
Of beaker form. Together they have made
A table, set for the carouse, it waits
For guests to sit. Already filled with wine
On it stand goblets thinly stemmed and fine
Of cut. These tulips were in yellow and
In red. Around them stood the hyacinths,
Bunched sombre dark-blue bloom, on stronger stem.
Log wood in moss on sod encircled them.
There hung, like 'neath the sea inside the woods
Of coral trees, still bits of dead leaves loose,
Turned brown. In them still shone the sun fire-red,
The flower colours though had just turned dead.

A village too could in that vale be found,
Where smoke of chimneys finely teemed around;
She saw that too. A shine in blue and red
The sun made on the tiles. Faint rumour met
The ear from a black smithy in the streets,
The iron clanked under the hammer beats.
They in a cadence hammered sparking flames.
The street was clear, she saw two neighbour dames
Who chatted in the door and a black stray
That walked around. Under green linden stayed
An old man while he watched the western sun,
A wife behind a house had just begun
The weeding. Then the school opened its door,

A train of children came, their pinafores
The girls wore chequered, clump of wooden shoes,
Meanwhile the shouts and yells of boys broke loose.
There were two fighting, others stood around;
The teacher came, then they were homeward bound
In twos and threes, the brothers hand in hand.
She saw them here and there go over land
And bridges and along a low hedgerow
And through the main street, suddenly they dove
Away into their homes, safe under ceiling.
It was then still again, save only steel cling
And clang and from a stall, dim lows of cows.
And in the main street she as well saw how
A bush of lilacs blew between the homes,
A pair of pigeons entered heaven's dome
On white wings clattering, and swam and danced
Around in rings before the steep expanse.

When she had seen it all and the bell tolled,
The air vibrated far and long, she strolled
Away as well and walked through pasturelands
Afar, the grass lay sprinkled full of glance,
Wet diamond dust. The rays of sun had touched
Like beard the dusky twinkling earth, it watched
Serene with gleaming eyes in flirt. A town
Of red and white stones lay there, drunk and drowned
In sunlight, which came through a granite gate
Into the streets of glass to saturate
Them to the brim. Did I myself not stand
In evening wind there, full of hay-scent, and
Did I not see that child under beech trees

Outside the gate? I'm doubting... maybe she
Passed during dreams my eyes in dusky acts
Of sleep-shadows. No, no, twas *her* in fact.
Did I not kiss you often my sweet May,
Down where the water passes by the way
Near those blue willow trees. Oh it was you,
So gentle felt your cheeks, skin of a puss,
And like a sea-shell your mouth closed round mine;
My blood the sea was then, you were my fine
Small ship that danced on my chest bearing it.
You seemed so secrets-filled, I asked you which
Ones do you want to read and in a damp
I felt them welling up. You were a lamp
To my hands, as to you I'd be the bee
To suckle your sweet honey, May, my sweet.

Sometimes it happens when fatigued at night
I'm trying to fall asleep, that streaming nigh
To me is your soft breath and flowing hair.
Your eyes are like two silent flames, in there
My head lies on my pillow; and while I
Dream off, they keep on burning in delight.
Like when you were a child and round your foot
Fumed flower scents and when that lightweight brood
Of cloudlets oversailed my head, and as
The moon was budding, Phoebus' bloom found rest.
I sat with you like at a tiny well
Of living water, where red play of elves
Takes place over the yellow sandy soils
And one can see the crystal bubbles boil.
You spoke so much all quiet and you gave

Me treasure troves of secrets which I saved
In stronghold. On my arms, warm child of grace,
You lay, blonde hair on red and fragrant face.
You made your lips just like a cherry round,
I ate so many kisses from your mouth.
You fled from my arm but I grabbed your hand,
And took you with me over my own land.

It was not very far but still seemed long,
For it was evening and there came a song
Deep from the vale where people lived, we stopped
Ofttimes and listened to them, now their job
Was done, delighted – and there came as well
A black bird through the air, but quickly quelled
Its colouring over the sunken sun.
And in the undergrowth, a small well sprung
And spoke to itself, a child, who, when he found
Us out observing him, made no more sound,
But laughs still rustled from far water-lands.
We also saw a nest, in which the hen
Sat with the rooster, eyes all closed and feather
In feather. But we hurried on together.

Till we arrived where scarlet blossoming
Of hawthorn filled the night. Wind did not bring
One cloud, so fragrance hung still full and tight
Around all branches. Here the dark would hide
Your face and we climbed onward through the sand
Into a deep dale, silent, hand in hand.
And here all things were wonder, and I well
Could wander here for ages or a bell

Of silver ring forever in this land.
There we lay down together. From my hand
She ate like bread the kisses and she bent
Just like a mother over me but sent
Her eyes no longer up, she then spoke too:
"My mouth is raining kisses and you, you,
My thirsty boy, you ask for always more
And still more droplets from this cloud. To your
Own town you should now turn." – And I long sat
In wait with pounding heart, and her soft head
Was touching mine – until she whispered: "Paths
Invite me everywhere, let me depart,
Seek now what is that scent, those glitterings;
Hear how the nightingale in thicket sings,
Where all the flowers stand between the grass,
A banquet of full chalices, each glass
And rummer foams up sweet and yellow wine."
She already seemed to drink when she let my
Numb fingers go. For a long while I stood
And watched how she drank empty in the wood
Most chalices of rose and violet,
In twilight shadows, grown in blue and red.

She found then, at the highest of sharp mounds
Of barren heather-hills, which formed a round
Fortification of a shallow hole,
A wall about a heath-camp like a bowl
With dark erica, not yet flowery.
She chased a bee that buzzed there hungrily
For honey, stepped into it, disappeared
From the red fire of the celestial sphere

That glowed beneath her arms. And there she sat
Down watching with wide eyes the unripe bed
Of grass shoots swinging back and forth, and which
Dared not offer resistance on that edge
To the calm evening air when it flew by
There on transparent wings but did excite
The little grass; and how surprised it was.
She saw how very slowly the blue glass
Of the expanse was fogged up by the dark,
The only red surviving was the spark
Of memory on the inflated rim
Of a red cloud – by day it had been cream,
But now it seemed a bed of violet,
Lying alone but saturated, wet
With lovely purple light, in empty land.
Beneath were rooting in earth's lower sand
White abele and birch trees, who, whispery,
Were trembling on the slope. For in those trees
Lived wondrous fright for twilight and for each
And every little wind that caught their leaves.
Oh there was much to hear that time of day,
Below there sauntered crooked gnomes and they
Removed their ancient books, out from the earth.
It's they who scour at night for stones the dirt
In which once druids chiselled medicine
And spell, a long time ago, against the pain
Of heart of youthful heroes. Also then
The pickaxe stroke was audible. And when
The western day had fully died, young elves
Emerged from their subsurface homes, they delve
In daytime gangways and a dusky mine.

Mineworker lamps are put around, their shine
Makes emerald halls in grass. And there resides
With parchment scriptures and in yellow-white
Habiliments, to study medicines,
An elf all night: what can heal gout; what reigns
Over pulse and heart. And past him, giggling
The elf-girls dance, their vestments fluttering
Much like a banner. It waved silently
While they made shuffles round the hill that eve.

Faint clamour stirred the gown of silken air
Even from far away. From bygone years
Some witches round the whole horizon steered.
They carry little children: May could hear
The sound of torture and the snowy rouse
Of trains of gowns back at her father's house.

The moon came and into the skies she sailed,
Just like an admiral who, clad in mail,
Stood fore on deck behind the golden shield.
The sails swell white on all the blue that wields
The seething salt in sprinkles of sea froth.
The fleet of stars gave way to both sides. Broad
Lay there the army road – like king-of-arms
The cloud gushed forward, in the coat-of-arms,
Its mistress' gold and white, it seemed to call
With trumpet brown and gold and cardinal.

Who possibly can handle that sun's blaze
When she stands naked, glowing white? Not May,
She could not, dreamt away. And all the while

At night, the moon watched her with golden smile.

And in the quivering twilight of the woods
Twelve little knights were trying if they could
Caress the moon's gold crumbling down black stems,
At first they are long strings, the wind on them
Strumming in woe, deep in the summer night.
They stretch while they descend on the dark might
Of forest, fracture in gold smithereens,
They touched twelve knights now in the forest greens.

They wore white mantles and a white tricot,
Berets plumed with white ostrich, they trod so,
The moon gleamed in their weapons, up the hill,
They gathered in a ring on top, stood still.

Those are the twelve night hours who're standing there,
So gently at the round moon's child they stare,
Like in a children's game in a small round,
In turn one breaks the ring and leaves that ground,
The others stay behind awake while he
Treads fast beyond the woods and the wide meads
And climbs the stairs into an ancient tower,
And for his comrades rings and tolls his hour,
They hear, in lavish gold of moon they see
Through trees his mantle glaring ivory.

That gilded night twelve knights were seen to stay,
Keep loyal watch around the little May.
The moon shone motionless and in a round
They stood there still, their rapiers in the ground.

II

There's a cathedral now that stands midland,
Of columns I piled up, around it bend
The weeping cypress and the poplar tree.
There's lily bounty, braids with rosy leaves
Are hanging down from every shaft, a string
Of children sitting side by side, they sing,
Red-cheeked on steps, throats open all the way;
An organ I hung on the wall to play,
Inside I placed the statue of a girl.
The only priest was I, that lavish world
Was mine, I lived there, solitarily.
The land was lonely by that sanctuary.
At night I waked in temple-shadow, blue
It gleamed, it waded in a sea of dew.
Onto the blue sky-brow the moon then flew,
Between those columns music gushed like dew,
Are they the birds, or are they butterflies,
Whose wings so musically flutterfly?
Or are they velvet feet of my dear May,
Who treads around the temple such a way
That skull-faced chains of flowery violets
Nod dreamily, the whole flower-school, at that?
Or maybe air had made these sounds by stirring
The wind and flower-swinging or the scurry
Of May who by the temple came to play.
Does not the air from bird throats in this way
Make sounds, does not the wind from trees and branches
Drive airy tones, as well from dress's fringes,

Does it not rustle meadows in the morning –
From air sprouts music when it's teeming, warring.

Just how could I abandon where my soul
Dizzied, far from my eyes light made its fall,
My eye and ear were like the firmament
Above the sea with teeming prism tint
Of water and music-balloons that mount
The seas, rise up from them, and with the down
Plucked from the wings of waves? And where the night
Enclosed the earth, and sprouted stellar white,
And smiled the heavens open with distinct but
Hushful looking at the black rich kingdom
Of earth, where the flowers with a sigh
Were born into the darkness of the sky,
The nightingale's lament exulted loudly
Above the flower that only just had sprouted?

I did not know this all so beautiful.
A girl may also bloom this way in full,
The groom walks round her to caress her hair,
His pointed fingers through her golden hair:
Then ignorant he leaves and seeks in play
Dullness and sleep. Then steps in his doorway
A naked image: 'neath the white bed-curtain
Glances are sliding followed by a word-train.
This is to cry for, as the daydreaming
About a thing's more tender than the thing.

I listen thus while playing, over meadows
From very far arrive just like word-shadows,

The dreams circling round me when I'm asleep:
Therefore, my sweet young sister, come to me.

Come now, my sweet young sister, come to me.
Too long the scythe has whizzed round you and me,
Blonde sister from our sunny grain come forth.
For hear, oh hear, there far away's been born
A sun-eyed brood, it dances and bears round
Music and incense, sister sweet come now.

See I now want to play sweet-sounding shawm
Once more, give me your hand and drag me on,
Teach your red feet to dance away with me.
There stands the temple. Do now rise and greet
Us all those children? Don't they seem like flowers
With fragrant rocking, hear, those names are ours
That they are calling, stay with them and stand there,
Yourself a flower, let me go and enter.

The quiet here. A twilight blue ascends
The wood-towers, sunlight glides, the leafage bends.
But now the organ will be playing, first
There will be music floating, then will burst
A waterfall: thus on the mountains stands the
American forest, the tree trunks banter
Each other who's the highest, blue sky surprised
Watches the leaves wave as each year they rise.
A river floats there in smooth plane and bed,
And mirrors rocks and trees, this floating wet
A forest-beast drinks when that streaming way
Starts shining from the coming break of day.

The stream goes murmuring through reed, which whizze
It breaks and then kinks down, over abysses
Pours rumbling out, stands after somersaults
Like a tambourine man who stirs the drum he holds.
This song shall lie so, across the countryside,
A thirsty people will drink at its side.
My soul flies off and bathes in loneliness
Through a tepid lake of clouds of happiness,
And slurps the blue air like the sweetest wine,
The ether mixed with sun's eternal shine.
My body wanders soul-sick, calls its bride,
Who lonely crosses clouds in fluttering flight,
It then sings wandering drunk this canticle,
You all hear – but *she* is ignorant of all.

The shadow sleeps along the mountains, their
Basalt is sad, a mountain's pale stream blares;
Night-clouds sail off and leave behind the skies.
It's quiet there, on earth are only cries
Of that one mountain, thick and tired's the air.
Round it the other mountains stand and stare.
May sits there, just awake, a pane of wine
Was purpling her limp dress, a branch of vine
Beside her, and with laughing light blue eyes
As if half asleep. But there's the sun who ties
Wagon to span, like leafy ivy rises
Rose colour past the skies, stars which are iced
In blue, melt down. Into her heart makes entrance
Most beautiful of people's slaves, remembrance.
How often she has now been listening
To the first bird song, when leaves jittering

And skittish flutter up for morning wind,
The swallow-flight and buzz of bees begins.
And then the air became so busy, now
She hardly heard the single sounds. See how
The first bird flies so fast, the water drips
In colours off the rock, the droplet slips
Along a flowery herb, with silver tail
A trout smashes the stream that falls away
With speed, oh, without sleep eternally.
How trembling now her hand and her pale cheek
Is watered by a blush, the slope her chest
Makes swells and strains the wine-stained dress?
It was the yester eve, when high up stars
Like chandeliers were hanging, and stood far
The low ones, which seemed armed like girandoles.
She sat here too then, purple and how low
The forest light, how silent-mute – abrupt
A voice rose like a fountain that erupts
Just once a year, makes cheerful-light its waiting
Water and then it's bursting-celebrating
Its own laughter; such was that voice and she
Turned frightened, melancholic, for it seemed
That voice had long missed something – still a treasure
Of jewels in daylight, like the sole possession
That a poor man keeps safe, after sundown
He goes there and exhumes it from the ground
And weeps and kisses it and only craves
To grit it to dust in fist; it must decay
Out of love-lust. 'T seemed now as if were heard
Coins rattling, then again as if were served
A twinkling wine, at night, from golden jug

Into a large bronze cooler. Quiet struck
Quite unexpectedly, now only shone
The moon. May had been standing though still long
With drinking ears and idle legs, until
She realised the silence, yelped a squeal
And turned very afraid. Yet joy returned
Then gradually, because she wished, she yearned
To hear it more, – does not the daydreaming
About a thing give comfort like the thing?

She had accelerated and she leapt
From rocks, then from a vine the stem she snapped
To make herself a staff; under her feet
From evening hours to the silent mid
Of night, the wood had cracked, the mountain stream had
Splashed, and it seemed as if there went a Maenad
Of Bacchus on the paths of arid rock
And blackened mountains. She was, as she walked
Out from the shadows, noticed by the moon,
She sat down in the light, then had been soon,
While panting from exhaustion, mimicking
That voice, but then she wept, head bent between
Dead leaves, if one still could it was not her.

She thinks this, and meanwhile the sun waters
The earth, it is the gardener of earth.
And small red flowers shimmered and reversed
Its rays with subtle colour-play, bright grass
Made waves like women's hair, whereas high trees
Started to rock the wind, much as a toddler
Who went to sleep while whining, still holds shut her

Eyes when she awakes and whimpers on,
The rustling wave of leaves amused her soon.
And reddish clouds were drifting like seaweed,
Back and forth, wandering erratically,
Peninsulas of sunny a horizon.
A glowing source, the earth lay vaporising:
Her open lips steamed with carnality,
Yellow with heat. But pouring lavishly
Were the stream-vases; Danube and the Rhine
This way pour out their water and cool wine.
And wind blew onto the earth's countenance,
The forests trembled at their mountain-stance,
Fatigued the granite dust and porphyry
Flew up, the golden foam of mountain stream
Flew with it, but it was not felt at all
In the green vales, by flower or mountain fall.

The skies filled so with windy noisery,
And bird throats with caressing voicery
Echoed along like brooks, rivers jumped out
From holes like animals, their lungs and mouths
Were growling. But the sunshine filled her eyes,
By it the ears are all but minimised.
Her eyes turned bigger, and a red glow burnt her
On neck and cheek, and there the red blood murmured,
And she could hear it only scantily.
The wind came on her like love-archery
With ointments and perfumes olfactory,
She smelled the incense, yet she let it flee.
Around her head the thoughts began to swarm
Like swarms of bees, in this chaotic storm

She could not hear one from the other; and
Her ears were buzzing as if many faint
Lips stood before her ears, as if all words said
Intensified her blush both sweet and matte.
It was as if those sweet words sailed and went
Around nicely in line but without sense
In her like little ships, upon her blood
Throughout her body, in an ample flood
Of warmth of heart. And she could not discern
Whether they came from outside like a burn
That flows into a lake, or if a well
Gushed them into the sun out of itself.
Before her eyes though lighted all things brilliant,
Tingled jumpily, like bells of silver
That have been rung aloud, her eyes then billowed
While they with tears and mistiness were filled.
Then she fell backwards from the stone, and down
With her came falling too her hair and gown.
Lust and desire, and gratification
Within her clashed in play and confrontation.
And so she lay amidst the world, it was
As if within herself a world she was.

She lay thus long, in her returned from yonder
Calmness, just like the summer after thunder;
A woman's heart like summer-meadow seems
Where cows are grazing peacefully in dreams,
Between them some don't graze and stand head-steady.
Her thoughts were much like that, she stared up at the
Blueish heaven-haze, and her whole head
Was dreamily warm, and summer-fruity red.

Quiet was all around, the noontime sun
Was twinkling, silence buzzed, and a bee hummed,
It spread its tender wings, on the rock face
The white sunlight had dried its midday rays.

The way the clouds after a winter day
Go grieving, although not one air-complaint
Is heard when it is silent everywhere –
Then I, while snow is falling here and there,
Can sometimes see a single cloud turn blush.
It travels laughing in between the bunch
Of crying clouds – and likewise were the reefs of
Sunlit mountains that go high in even
And sloping hillsides, turning blue and grey.
On it appeared amidst snow-ice and blaze
Of dust and rock, a body in fair-red
Of a young god, his feet together treaded
In turn and forth, around his high head fanned
The bushy hair like sun-spark spraying vent.
Around his neck and throat a chain of value
In gold, his nose steamed breathing like a stallion.
He seemed a sun but red and lovelier
Than sun itself, with red light of the star
Of Mars midwinter night, yet around him
By his own light, there was no shadowing.
He walked and hummed, the air would turn insane
When he breathed in and with a drag he strained
His lungs to fill such that his chest was puffed.
Then he exhaled, made even mad the dust
With tingling, all in wait the heavens longed –
Until he gradually started his song:

Where the wind is and eternal gush
Round Wodan's house of water's rush,
     Where the sea is light
     And the dark of night
Glints with the stars, which are like dust.

Where late in the hurricane of night,
In the waxing moon as wax so white,
     The goddess choir
     Round the altar fire
At the Ocean in a dance unites.

Where thunderstorms when blown
Leave forest trees like mown,
     Where the rumble-cow lows,
     Upwards once more grows
The pinewood that Wodan has sown.

Where Aurora wraps her child in binds,
Ray-wreath that makes the night-time blind,
     And with ringing tings
     And with tinkling rings
It begins to walk while light it shines.

There I once lived, woe me, oh me,
Then dreamt the young Idun with me
     With her bare little toes
     In the red of roses
Of the cloud-spread thin and cottony.

Who brought the platter, then in gold, red wine,
For Wodan and Freya, at the meal divine
      To his rocky height,
      Where in royal pride
They presided in the hall to dine?

Who took the moon-mare from the stall,
And walked with her through heaven's hall,
      That those swans like twins
      In that swarm of wings
Flap-fly everywhere with all?

Who hunted forth the sombre riders,
Crowded clouds, to solicide,
      Who let their hailstorm blow
      As if with sabre blow,
Riding from their northern sites?

Who built one eve the palace of the west
That through cloud-ice with coal-fire flashed,
      From cloud-pumice whirls
      And some spumish pearls,
Where the gods flew in for journey's rest?

Who milled the sun so that the golden bliss,
The sun-flour, fell, who gave the hitch
      To the solar wheel
      That splashed the sea,
And milled the morning-waves to bits?

All that did Balder, I,
No blink of an eye
I sat depressed
In shadow and in distress,
Or did I cry.

He went and sang, while May sat very still.
He stood then, turned to her, and shivers spilled
Over her arms and she had to sustain
Herself with both; her dress hung in a train
And trembled on her feet whereas her hair
Hung round her forehead, the blue vein waved there;
Her eyes pervaded all her face turned white
And pale, although the sunlight made it light.
And blind she turned with open eyes, for when
He stood so stirless, he once more began;
Like silver spider-web his voice was spinning:
She saw it tingle, he was melting in it:

Awoken as I once awoke,
I am like that now, it was on the sand
By the wide gold-sea that in evening soaked
In the high torching sun of the god-land.

Didn't I the swaying see,
Like leaves of poplar trees,
Of goddess hair, hands on the other shore?
And did not gleam the stars,
Oh it came from far, so far,
That as a hairband Idun wore?

Like this I fell asleep,
Around me grazed my sheep,
I heard their teeth when reed was yanked,
In moist of clouds it grows
Where swirls of heaven flow,
A lullaby in there the wind-bride sang.

Alas when I woke up,
Just while Aurora dropped
The cradle-binds loose from the child of sun,
My eyes were then wound tight,
And hardly any light
Or tint out from those blinded sources sprung.

And I then sailed away
Onto the rustling waves,
For all I knew it was heaven-light sea,
I floated listening
To dim sea-whispering,
My tears flowed with the salt serenity.

And I have roamed around,
Where grey a desert ground
In the bright moonlight lonely wastes away,
And there my cheeks acquired,
How great was my desire,
The earliest of red in morning rays –

And I have then ascended
To where the rain commences,
The dew of clouds dripped on my eyes and down,
And I sucked honey-clouds
In Iris' rounded house,
No thing to drench my blindness I have found.

Twilight to see,
A reverie,
Who calls the name of what caught me?
Ringing tings,
Tinkling rings,
I heard when they opened the gate for me.

Angel sentries
Asked me gently
For my name I pondered then.
Twilight to see,
Tinklings repeat,
Evaporated memory.

There's missing hence
Reminiscence
Of want and sadness that I always wore,
What's not vanishing
Is the replenishing
With music-drink always and always more.

It is the soft waving arriving
Of the blue-feathered diving
Of doves along sunrays out of the sky –
It is the bobbing closing in
Of the blue baldachins,
Swollen with a fiery southern sigh.

It is the getting tender nourishing,
It is the nightly flourishing
Of a flower secret but delightful –
It is the breathing filling
With the scents that veil in
A wonder-dream a wide world.

It is glorious the revelation
Of hazes, in which teems a congregation
Of men and women in sunlight transparent –
It is watching clear as day
For shapes that don't give way
Like mountains of a hard granite and diamond.

They are the fiery nights
With moon and star the guardian knights,
A hollow air filled with a lunar glint –
As blazing as a victory,
So stands the sun in its glory
By every dawn and on that battlement.

It is the swaying as the wheat ears swing,
It is the sounding of the guitar strings,
It is the music as it weaves and spins –
It is the music-curtains' tremoring,
It is the tone-trains' rolling in,
They're music-clouds for sweeps of wind.

A background's shifting full of wonders now,
It is the bursting as it loudly thunders out,
Breaking and smacking of black summer nights,
It is an evening sea, of wave-bells full,
Ringing below the clouds, and they are pulled
Forth by the dark and swimming naval might.

Oh, they are the caravans
Of music, and the desert sands
Become oasis-avenues they're playing on,
It is the slide continuous
Of my music-galleass,
At sea with golden copper in the blazing sun.

Come all, anywhence
Flowers and incense
You bring for my pale and quiet loneliness –
Now I want to sling
Many silver rings
Of small songs from my loneliness.

        There is not one[5],
        No, no, not one
Who knows like me its desert lands –
        It is my vault,
        My father's hold,
My town, my heaven tent.

She had her knees pulled up high, that was where
Her arms were leaning, while her light blonde hair
Enwrapped them, and her hands both held concealed
Her cheeks and eyes, which too themselves were sealed
And shut; it seemed she was alone and dwelled
High up in heaven, deeply sunken felt
Below the whole wide world and far away
Remembrances of any life of May.
How light was all and what a tingle-show;
Was it quiet, or not? She did not know,
Her heart and wrists were beating to the song
Still, and around all air-sparks sang along.
Then in her hands she saw an image-throng
Flicker along, as if in their trained robes
White shapes were wading through light-flows.
Some wore their instruments, the strings aflare
Between rose-fingers, trumpets too, the bare
And wide-mouthed ones, which men held to their mouth.
That was her cheerfulness, she'd just devoured
Her tears, when hastily before the wind
Of her reflections, in his rosy tint
The singer himself came out, in his light
They all escaped and vanished from her sight.
He sang first and his mouth seemed like the lair

Of winter-midnight heaven, when the air
Is full of precious stars, his songs released
What seemed a rain of stars, a company
Of white tones came out sparkling from his mouth.
But it became more silent and the sound
Was gone. He stood up straight and still before her,
His mouth and eyes were closed, no sign or stir.
At first her thoughts remained like birds and shy
Round him, they did not have the nerve to fly
In his body's illuminated wake.
But already braver they began to sway
Closer, and then her eyes went off and on
His broad chest, which just like a road ran down.
And pure just like a golden holy sculpture,
He flamed in darkness, which seemed like a bulwark
Of black rock. And it did make her forget
If really it was dark, that flaming statue
Blossomed so much, to flowers more akin
Than cruel fire, much as if his skin,
Just like rose leaves wrapped as a covering,
Cloaked a red spark, of which had leaked the glint
From the inside of the leaves. She stretched her hands,
Palms up ahead and lake-like coruscated
Her shining eyes and soft desire pervaded
Her lips and with a delicate caress
She seemed to touch him. – Play though had egressed:
He was not there. High in its yellowness
The sun was burning and her eyes were closed,
In her soft face now by her hands enclosed.

The sun was sinking and the dales turned dark,
The awesome evening wandered round, and sparks
Began to glint in heaven-cities, and the peaks
Of mountains, late still lit, received oblique
The rays of sun. Like this the evening streets
Of cities are half-dark within our states
Of Holland, on the eastern side, in turn,
Cream-yellow and wall-red, and windows burn.

The night set in. The child sat high and bent,
The earth mused stout and still. And there ascended
A plump and fluffy vapour, pale and nodding
Like anemones, for they as well stand tottering
In the watery depths of sea. And she
Became all wet and damp-cold when that sheath
Cloaked over her, and when a fluid cap
Of flakes of vapour drowned her head. The flap
Of her woven dress over a stone had dropped.
The vapour drips were lying there, the sobs
Of air, fair-black like Cape Land diamond.
She did not weep or twitch, but at the seafront
Of her own grief she sat and saw waves climb.
Her mother knew, she sat on the horizon,
Waiting by her watch-fire, just awakened,
Now by her dark-blue bed and mother-naked
She stood and saw her child, and from her eyes
Came melting beams, the vapours moved aside,
And then her blonde and yellow hair she stirred.
The air turned hazy: and when by a surge
Of her white light the stars were overflowing,
Midst greenish haze the little moon-child shone.

Her feet she placed several times in all
Without a splash deep in the haze. A bowl
Of silver she scooped full with fire, which showed
Her face in light, her body dark below.
And so she came towards her child, and bright
Her shine glowed very high before the wide
Bow of the heavens. Like a tigress that
Searches her cub in cliffy desolate
Wasteland, she came there and she noticed her
Sitting, arm enfolding knee, and over her
She stood, colossal. Neither of them spoke
A word, not high up there or down below.

They thought of the same thing, just like a mother
Who lives the children's life, in time of bother
Brings welcome help to them. They both did think
That merriment was finished, suffering
Was now being prepared. But still the young girl
Was relishing it, for the youth will conquer
Legions of pain and take the fortified
City of future with their hope. Surprised
She gauged the depth still of her loneliness,
Found comfort in wonder, how limitless
The loneliness, now that he filled no more
The day… where would he be? … Once more before
Her eyes she saw him rise as pure as gold.

Not so her mother. Because soft and cold
A shudder blew over her limbs. To a mere
Akin that ripples in dark moors, her dreary
Skin was shaking, trembling and her head

Shook her lock-load about. A lioness
Whose dearest cub was robbed, first from despair
She's stirless, then roars loudly. Thus she stared
Ahead a little while, then groaned. Storm's thunder
That from afar was heard. Like the swan's feather
In windy gust, May darted up and forth so,
In front of her she saw dark feet, the torso
Through the sky darkening to her and bright
The face, now forward bent and heaven-high.
It came downwards and in the glittering
Of mother gleamed the child. And captured in
The light, her breast and arms she opened wider.
And mother, stooping, put the bath of fire
Upon a mountain slope and the rose leaf,
Her child, she then held close, round her curved knees
Her one arm, while the other one relieved
The column, her fine neck, and down sat she.
The chandelier lit fiery, lavishly
The child impressed the lips into her breast.
It seemed an infant that with thirstiness
And with eyes closed, out of her mother drinks.
She opened them and asked: "Mother, what blinks
So much there, makes the vapour-twilight seem
Like smoke of fire? Oh, put out all that gleam
Of light now, let me kiss you in the dark."
Her mother blew the fire out, from the arc
Between the mountains vapour surged once more,
Like horsemen when they stand on ground of war
Anticipating the command, who when
That comes ride forth, hoofs striking, and back bent.

And when they had for long kept silent in
The secret chamber of that vapouring –
The moon stood watch in there, like governess
Of lands in Scandinavia, princess
May let her eyes sleep full and lavishly
With allegories, but in pageantry
The mother-eyes were shining – then began
The Moon, like moon-stream that through wood-lanes ran
"My child, what are your thoughts, what lights your eyes:
She wallowed in her arms and drank her light
Of eyes in gulps and sheltered closer yet,
And said: "I see before the stars your head,
Mother, and in your head two eyes, concealing
Vapour though floats about, where they stand really
I do not know, oh like a whirl that's filled
Lukewarm with bathwater, it tastes like milk
Inside my mouth I milked one early morn.
Still I am thirsting, mother, – and the dawn
Is, I believe, still far, its lucid peaceful
Silence – for light and sun as pure as sea salt.
Mother, I so much loved those, will this hot
Dull head be mine for good now and my blood
So, drunken, buzz around? Oh full am I
Of blood that's dark as wine dregs, where could hide
Herself my former self then, the fair May?
I smell such heavy scents, my eyes are weighed
Down by a heavy black-red canopy.
Oh mother, help me now, what can this be?"
She answered and it was just like the breeze
That blows after sun-midday: "Will I see
You so once more, my dear blonde daughter, how

Golden and blonde were you, yet you are now
Tired and all too warm and red. But wait,
I'll make you snow again, your body made
A hall of youth and strength and calm and cool."
She stooped over and breastfed her. The stool
Of rock bore mute that heavy goddess-pair,
The Moon and May, while her abundant hair
Clouded the mother womb. And almost slum-
Bering she suckled in the haze – as from
A cask, milk siphons to a droughty barrel –,
From mother's nipple to the mouthly chalice.
She thus found calm in saturation. Long
She stayed and lay there while the vapour hung
Over the deep abyss, just now and then
The mother blew a sigh, just like a man
Who's pondering. And thus she finally spoke:
"Mother, I love you, and I wanted oh
So dearly now to follow you, always
Be with you. – But now something separates
Us, you and me. And I would not obey
Always your summoning and when the shade
Shadowed your realm, I would be capable
No more to stay. Where the far spectacle
Of heaven would be red, the loneliness
And light I'd search. Mother, what happiness
It brings to me that I know his delight,
Shall I not seek him there now until I
Stand in front of his house? On the doorstep
I'll be kissing his footprint and perhaps
I'll hear the resonating of his voice.
Mother, his songs are columns, don't they shore

Stout marble palaces in blinding white?
In there are chambers coloured by red light,
Is he not at the end and waits and waits?
See, I stand on the doorstep, see he waves
At me and laughs, yes now he'll be my king.
Here am I, here am I, can I live in
This home forever? Oh, I'll make it fine.
It is already fine, see all the finery,
Summery flowers dangle, wintery crystal,
Covered with ice and with burgundy coral
Are the walls, oh I bury myself in roses."
Then startled she refrained and changing pose
She laughed still more a bit, her mother didn't.
She spoke though, like through reed and rush the wind:
"The waterfalls and silver streams do too
Depart the mountains, and the forest woods
Give up each year again their dearest leaves.
My children once were to me like a sheaf
Of ears, now so many have gone and vanished.
Where are they? I don't know, it's long since any
Of their smooth limbs were dancing on my earth.
She also holds you dear and she preserved
Treasure for you, multi-coloured, thousand-kind.
You don't want it? Then please leave me behind."

Just like a ship at sea, she pushed away,
She like a ball of air descended, gave
No longer shine, in dark she walked the earth.
Until she reached a lake that faintly stirred
And waved a little in the dark of night.
She stood there looking over it and cried,

An alcove over water the black sky.
Small stood a poplar next to her, despised
The silence, and now also softly flustered.
Her tears were rustling, leafage whooshed and sputtered.

And she seemed dead. On girl's feet May approached
So softly, and sweet as dessert she coaxed
Her with these words: "Oh do not be annoyed
Mother, I beg you, for whichever choice
I make from what you give, will turn me so,
Just so unhappy, ever since a beau
So splendorous and tender spoke to me.
You don't know, did not hear, a single tree
I'd creep on like a snail, now that on wings
I see a world a day and in a sprint
Can reach the top of golden pyramids,
The great world, where the vapour seethes amidst
The hottest boiling happiness, where I
Will see him back, if just a wink of an eye.
You too were seeking, with your light, blue caves,
And carried one there and then held your ray
Focused so he could slumber, didn't you know
That through the leaves there gleamed his arm and throat?
Mother, remember youth, when from the sun
You too were hiding with Endymion."
She stooped and slowly lifted up her child
And looked at her, kissed her, and for a while
She did not move, then put her on the ground.
And May walked forth, a child, in the lake's surround
The Mother was still standing, stayed, a tree.
Round her flowed vapour-wind, the boundary

Of dark land sometimes being overstreamed
By mirky water, like a man by dreams.

That night no one did see her, soft round May,
Not the capricious satyr or the race
Of Fauns that on the hills go out to play.
And not the elves with dresses long with trains
Behind each other like a caravan
That's strolling through the mist to understand
In great assembly and decide, what can
Be done next morning till in heat that ends
At noon, when children of the elves will sleep
In lily leaves that cloak the water strip.
The glistening stars were looking curiously,
Chatter of linden leaves, wind jauntily
Blew through the woods with joy, none else to see.
Mountain or valley, none knew where was she.

But when the sun blossomed, and morning winds
Blessed the leaf-woods – she loped to doe akin
From a cool forest. Naked, with foam-drops
From when she fell; and like from a cold tub
Thundered behind her loud a cataract.
She held her ground where on the plain are stacked
The trees around the rocks like city wall.
There she stood, like a flower she stood tall,
Like flower-fragrances came out her words:
"Father, when you arise you fill the skirts
Of heaven with your light, you will make shine
The dark night-clouds just like abundant mines,
Golden and silver, oh my father, total

Well-lust, spring-source, from whom the fountains flow
With all the light, give also shine to me.
I'll stow it in my eye, with twinkling glee
Due to your hidden light, and my blonde hair
Grows up from there, just as the wheat grows where
The golden seed fell and the summer rain.
Give, give it to me, now that the new ways
I'll travel – Mother also gave me milk."
He heard her, and he let light pour and spill
In her fair body through each opening.
The light was pure as gold, but her fair skin
Was like a sieve, twas purer still inside
Of her, it spread outwards like glister-light:
Rose buds collect their light this way, the rose
Burns with it till it dies – and when the glow
Of light had burnt a while and what was heavy
In her had been consumed, she felt like feathery
Herself, plumage of birds. And to a child
Of morning chill and of the wind of night,
That on a tree branch high above was sleeping,
She asked, complaining sweetly, early cheeping
Of a wakening small bird that its voice still seeks:
"Call your father now, would you, where is he?"
It whistled, lifting higher its small head,
A subtle sound, and from the east, the red,
Flew Morningwind to her on a great wing,
A wind-horse trotted next and reined to him.
She said: "I wanted where the clouds go sail
Will-less on wild wind, there I'd want to dwell."
She said this laughing, – and he looked at her
And panted with his horse in leaves that were

Iridescent and while the horse manes chilled
He said: "I was where flower-barrels spilled
Their scent, the sun its light, oh you are more
Than flowers and sun, I'll leave you nevermore.
May I be jiggling you, may I be sizzling
Around your ear where clouds are dizzying?
Don't fear, I mean no harm, I'll lead you forth."
He laughed, their eyes shone, like the bleating of
A little lamb she spoke her gratitude:
"I do thank you, but let the path I choose
Be mine alone, stay here, and let your breath
Caress me, that you may." Her voice arrested.
He nodded somewhat sadly. But he saw
Her laugh, and mirrored then her laugh once more.
Then he went forth, blew from an open place,
A forest square, his blowing all the way;
The tender air blew flowing up in scud,
The wind-stallion neighed round the earth in rush.

Like on a sofa, though that wasn't here,
She drifted forth, first through the lowly sphere
Of butterflies – a swallowtail sat well
Up in a tree near a flower-home, "Farewell,
Farewell" were lisping May-lips very gently.
And then, inside her entered eyesight's sentries,
Tiny white soldiers that had deep inside
Her head their guardhouse, she watched tranquilised.
An instant. It turned cooler and then she
Noticed the clouds close by her, tenderly
She spoke: "I recognise you, horses fine."
It was a complete herd, they did not shy,

But rather shook and plunged their heads or reared.
Slowly they drifted forth, she with them, steered
Through open heavens, just like smoke that could
Not climb the chimney, tarries where the wood
Sprouted in flames, and lingers there and stays,
Loving the people's room. "Oh do not chase
Me out yet," hardly audible, May murmured.
The wind did hear it and the air-disturber
Halted its breath, and all things stood. The sun
Then shone with hotter rays, pulled up and on
The clouds and ever higher, likewise pull
The fishermen the net and up the fishes-zoo,
Slowly it passes through a lot of fish.
Some of the clouds appeared to her like fleece
Of soap-sud bubbles, and drifting through those
Were stripes and colour-circles, deep below
She saw some heavy black ones like a wave
Grown high before a storm and far away
A flask with white steam hung, which turned and rolled.
The sun shone fiery now; like from a bowl
That in the heath forms after a squall in summer –
When dark the hills look down, the paths that slump
Along it are submerged – there from the sky
Strikes light and soon it has the pool acquired,
Rippling in white, it drinks the water – and
Likewise, the sun devoured the cloudy band;
Only some ragged haze remained, that whirled
Away far in the scenic spectacle.

And higher drifted she like that red bird,
The Nile flamingo who is also lured

By the gold orb, the sun, and his curved neck
Lies in his carmine wings and golden flecks
Leak sliding down his white-red feathered rim.
Such was her drifting and such her soft skim
Over the beachless surface, fluid brim.
And always rising. The blue ceiling seemed
To go higher and swelling, while the earth
Completely lay below like a hot hearth
With mottled flames of green and vapour-white.
How blue it was round her, above, her ride
Without a swinging and without a close.
She fanned her fingers sometimes, oft a rose
In quiet garden shakes her leaves like that.
The day was night-still and the solar head
Prepared his hairdo like a golden tent.
Sometimes she rose up and then made a stand,
Laughing against the silence like a clock.
Then she lay down again and pulled in snug
And like a child all dreamily her knees,
Then fell asleep till woken by her dreams.
Finally, she lay on her back, she wrought
No more, then in that atmosphere she thought,
And thought aloud: "I now would wish that he
Above came here and far with him brought me.
Likewise, I once have seen a single lamb
Remain in dunes in the wake of its sheep-gang
In the evening and time and time again
While it was grazing, bleating it looked round,
Homesick, but bowed its head then once more down.
I too will wait content, one way or other
I will be close to him. Thank you." Her father

Nodded at her, like flower coming nightfall
That nods goodnight towards the breeze. The idol
Of heaven, sunlight, gaily shook its hair.
She lay thinking and speaking on the air's
Stretcher for long: a woman often thinks
Her wish and speaks it, living on the fringe
Between reality and twilight zone
Where Hope sings night and day her magic song.
She sleeping-dreaming drifted on: a ship
Lonely at sea, that from the wave's smooth lap
Climbs over from that wave into another –
They're dancing cheerfully next to each other.
Thus seemed the air in its beatitude
Of smoothened silence too, infinitude
Of ether did not yet start there, but in
Most utter fineness a cloud-ring drifted in.

She saw that in the eve – all lay deep blue,
The sun had set – a city that's produced
By cheerful Moors in Spanish areas.
With a light stroke swelled up the cupolas
Like by paintbrushes and the minarets
Stood much like slender girls. And in a jest
Without a sound, arcades bowed on and on,
In endless corridors; and halcyon
Hung there a twilight in a saturation
Of light and of airy gratification.
She drifted there, through the white corridors
She bobbed, a soft and breathing longing born
From her spread out, filled the poriferous
Cloud-marble with its warmth, decisionless

Meanwhile she sailed ahead. Past parlour walls
She rose to the transparent trembling hall's
Ceiling, through opened window kept on gazing.
Blank was the world where every congregation
Of heavenlings together navigated,
The line of stars, as once were allocated
Their place and order by a major God.
Then she once more descended, till an odd
Most wonderful mosaic touched her feet,
She settled her red body down in it:
Music she thought to hear, it blew her forth,
Back up again – in summery resort
The wind plays so with rose leaf that's blown loose.
An open hall then lured her, there by a smooth
Wall flared heaven-blue a lucid fire,
The floor reflected it, like morning sky
At dawn awakened in a placid pool.
There too sat airily on fragile footstool –
All things seemed haze and twilight – a lightsome virgin,
Made from a blush and laughs, sometimes swerves in
A cloud at daybreak thus before the sun.
A spinning wheel in front of her, she spun
Hundreds of threads, which were like water-rays,
How they in silver ears originate,
From the black rock into a waterfall.
They streamed forth and they floundered from the hall
Into the arcades – hundred-mouthed a brook.
And May went in, stayed in the door, there looked
The spinster, wondering-laughing, up and at her:
May asked: "What do you spin, what are those threads?"
In murmuring words the maiden answered that:

"I am the cloud-spinner out of the north,
I spin the finest clouds, that float, trot forth
The highest, blossoms from the harvest reaped
By sunlight in the daytime from the sea.
The finest reaches highest, I collect
That in a clew, see how the scalawag
Now by a herd is followed from my hall.
They're grazing everywhere innumerable."
Right then a vapour-window opened in
The wind, and both looked out and saw walking
And climbing sheepy cloudlets, white in coat,
Like out at sea the waves in foamy coats.
Some strayed away, they seemed to dream and wander
Around alone, and stared into the yonder.
Most went together in an equal step,
As soldiers pace without an overlap.
And she spoke from the blue and burning flame:
"You'd like to wait here till the break of day?
Come here then, and sit down with me and tell
About yourself, I spin, but hear you well."
And May came closer, she lay down unwound
Close by the spinster's little foot, the sound
Then started streaming with the rustling course
Of vapour-threads passing that sluiceway door.
"I have the sweetest name, my name is May,
You heard of me, I think, for none remained
Among all of the elves and water-nymphs
And field-gods and the white and crimson winds
And each one of the airborne eminences
Who did not know my name, they would present me
With any gift at all for any kiss.

But kissing gave me heartache so I vanished
Often, but ever angry there was none.
All I desired did I and everyone.
I have only one wish now and that soon
Will too, I think, bear fruit. Would ever bloom
In me wish-blossom, then immediately
Ripe fruit would also hang abundantly."

She for a while kept silent, then resumed:
"There's one I seek, I only can presume
Where he can be, I fiercely want to learn,
You maybe know." The other said in turn:
"What is his name, he's one from earth below?
I'm never there. But if it's here he roved
Around, sooner or later I'd see him."
May spoke: "The morning and the bird that sings,
You don't know them, over the spotless mead?
Evenings in lonely groves along the heath
The nightingale and after, all day long,
The rattling of the leaves, laughs that belong
To all the earthly waters' glint and glow?
You don't know them, then hear his name and know
The spring and laughter, me and my May-childhood.
Balder, his name is Balder." And she cried out
That name in joy, and its resounding roll
Cleared all the vapour from the heaven-hall.

And when the other had heard this, she cried.
When she could cry no more, she thus replied,
The eyes of both meanwhile iridescent
With tears, blue flames around made their ascent:

"Balder, his name is balm and just like dew.
The open ears of a young dame like juice
Drink him in, fill the body then deep down
With his abundant name, its wealth and sounds.
Because she has the head filled to the brim
With that sound, in her eyes is shivering,
Behind, his image wildly flickering,
She seeks him too, I know, she's picturing
To find him in advance, oh I know well."
And then she cried again, much like a well
That overflows and makes a soggy ground.
The loom stood still, last weaves already bound
To leave the door. They sat like this for long,
Both dreaming, in that way a single song
To one gives hope, one else memorial
When it is heard, it's wonder-wonderful.

Vapour turned pink and red, midst fading blues
The sun appeared and soddened the white fumes
In golden rays: the two of them stood up,
Two lambs alike, that stand on a hilltop,
After their sleeping, slowly waking up.
May held the other's hand, through blazing of
The lavish light along a narrow hike,
A brim of clouds, a coastal beach just like
By Holland and the sea, in sandy whites.
Until they halted jointly, both with eyes
Turned to one side, and then one maiden said to her
Comrade "Do you see there where the feathers
Of this cloud penetrate the endless ocean
And stick out like a jetty? It's the roadstead

From where you have to go. I leave you now."
Then they towards each other turned around
And this one kissed the other on the mouth.
Then they rotated from each other round,
And wandered parting, hardly could the one
Restrain her feet, meanwhile the other spun.

There lay the air-sea teeming silently,
A sea of atmosphere, the heavenly
Ether lay pale above it, there stood she,
And flickering rustled a sea-melody.
She then remained and sat there all the day
And night, with that one image holding sway
Over her while her breath was warm and humid.
She was so full of him, forest in brume is
Thus filled with vapour on an autumn day.
But nothing else is moving there, the day
Knows only moving mist and misty tone.
Sometimes she wept a while, then would be flowing
Out of her mouth a murmur, as wild chickens
Sound often in the shadow of the thicket.
She had no single thought and not a word
Can therefore tell what she was thinking, heard
Can't be the parts most tender of a soul.
And as the earth will be when the rain falls,
A summer rain that's dripping with a rustle,
Hours and hours, such that a warming bustle
Fills the whole forest 'neath high canopy
Of heavily stemmed trees and heavenly
The flowers with that dew from grass will swell –
Just so the innermost of that young girl

Was infinitely large and chock-full with
The dawning of her hope, there could not live
Anxiety just where an amply sized
Abundance of that presence was devised.

She did not know she was somewhere, although
Her eyes were open and light vapour rolled
In waves in front of her, she did not see them
Though, or how the lustrous night succeeded
The day, the day the flickering of the night.
She was alone completely, supervised
Her soul just by herself, watched what went in
And round and out then from that magic ring.

While she guarded herself thus pondering,
Two youthful gods at sea were closing in
In competition and on flickering foot.
Their laughter May could hear, it was like toot
And hoot on hunting horns when they passed her
In front and swung around and made a whir
Of oscillation in the sunlight rays.
Just as two cyclists do: they make rotate
The steel of wheels, which splash around the light,
Circles are turning and the white path slides
Away: they pedal steadfast while they glance
At each other's wheels, each in their heart resents
With animosity, the goal one wins,
Once more the other overtakes still, in
Despair he passes blindly. The final step
Releases people's cheers and their hands clap –
They scurried onward so, once more abated

The sunlight. Then May looked and stood up straight
Inquisitively, breathing deep at first
As if just awoken, felt renewed a thirst
That like a sea breeze blew around in her.
Then she took wing and off the cloudlet-berth
To space and through the sunlight transited,
For nothing else was there, she targeted
The hurry of her feet at darting gods.
They went much faster though and quickly trod,
The messengers and envoys in god-land,
Yet long she saw them, still when gone the scent
Of oils she smelled, which from their shoulders oozed
And melted in the sun to fumes, diffused
More broadly then, they made their fragrant way.
And May resembled now the water snake
That swims across the ditch, the body a tail
That serpentines, and then a mackerel
That speeds through water in a blue-scaled gown.
And then a magpie underneath the crown
Of clear wood in descending, rising flight,
That screeches with loud voice in blue and white.

Until she came to where the flame-phalanges
Burn like in battle, seeming orange fences
Of fire, as centuries-old forests tall.
There crackled nothing, silently new squall
Of flames rose time and time again from old:
Flames just like palm leaves and like fans of gold
That in a ballroom by the walls may stand.
Columns of fire like when into the land
Invades the enemy and in the night

The still black mountains all to great surprise
Burst now with fires from mighty bivouac.
She flew into the fire, like hole and crack
In ice it spread, on which blows eastern blaze.
She went through fire-arbour some, amazed
She heard tongues that were lisping and made whooshes
Of words as if from tree leaves, but the sluices
Of flames let her go out of there, this just when
She planned to stay and listen to what's rustling.

And she swam further like a mighty fish
That quiet and in deeper water is.
Her eye was deep and cold, a wonderment
Awoke beneath in her, quite odd or quaint.

Then she came to the heaven's hanging drapes
Of silk and sun, like in the passageways
That can be found between the Chinese halls:
Figures spun in there were strange animals,
Like griffins, vampires, and the blood-red dragons
With wriggling tongues in jaws with teeth and fangs.
She saw the legs move slowly when they swayed
Open in a blow of wind, the silken bays
Of drag-curtains displayed slow ostentation
Expanding on their waves, with it the nation
Of animals blew high, quite endlessly:
A movement very far, and soundlessly.
In colour green and violet, pink-red
Swelled alternatingly the sail, thus sets
A fleet of ships its course and trims the sheets.

She hurried past them, there was nothing she'd
See clearly, because the exertion made
Her eyes blind, filled her head, music then played
At once around her, it was cordial.
She turned her head, now here, then there, fearful
And glad, but saw not much, a single bloom,
An eglantine, and sometimes roses loomed
While darkly lurking in a rosy bush.
It was more flowery now, but open, loose,
Already it gave way, no thing was close;
Above and round her hung a fragrant row
Of luminous musical flowers, far peal
From heavy waters, everywhere revealed
Itself a single bird, all shrill they sang.
Laboriously she steered forth, felt strangled,
Constricted round the arms, and suddenly
Set free, facing a brook-veined flower field.
A source like a cooling vessel there foamed over,
A brook sprang from that bed and through the open
Pastures, it roamed and grazed its little ripples.
And making music, angel-elves there dipped
Their legs in water, by the riverfront –
Triangles sounded, strings with flatter drone.

Further, further, the meadow turned to heath,
With darker soil, and sunlight's melody
Was evermore inaudible, a grand
Eve looming lazily, in darkness drenched
The eyes of May who seemed now like a bat,
That swarmed around night-sick in shadow-stead.
She rowed now slowly into the obscure

That lay before her, whispering it lured,
Absorbed her in between its folds and tucks.
New miracles, because a ghostly flock
Of giants shifted forth in it, and herded
A drove of mammoths, which made darkness stir
As mountains do after the earth has shocked.
They were with heavy arms and heavy locks,
They breathed out vapours, vapoury themselves.
They trekked about, not hastily, themselves
And others they pushed forth with heavy grumble
And a shout, while a forest sounded rumbles,
Or so it seemed, of falling trees of oak.
An emptiness and silence. Then a smoke
Of savage clouding haze she saw soar in,
And out rode troops of horse riders warring,
With heavy blankets hung on black horsebacks.
Clubs fell and people fell – revenge attacks
Were croaking, surly cries ascended – Valkyries[6]
Were driving forth those fighting and wide vultures
Were clouding after them. – All noises stopped
And with dull leaf-shivers a wood grew up.

And through those dreams of gods, a dream-hedgerow,
While lighter it became, she sought her road;
She still saw in the distance beings near
Between the trees: grandfathers with grey beards
And fair-haired women through the whitish damp.
She fled from them and sought the open camp,
She saw it through some light-green foliage.
The forest faded as though on a long bridge
A rolling wagon-train was vanishing.

All seemed future there, and reminiscing
No one ever did: a new delectation
Opened the gates: in her anticipation?

In front of her a blank street, water-flat
Between two mainlands, there a tower stretched
Up on the other side and white as snow,
Built out of blocks of ice, from furrows flowed
Over these blocks ice-water, yellow falls:
In every block the sun shone, and from all
The tower the water-gold came down and spilled;
And heaven-high the tower had been built
Till deep into the blue, but lower at
The battlements was where great pigeons sat
With smooth beaks, which caressed in their smooth feathers
And naked men were sitting there unfettered
By vertigo, and blew the clarion.
A tower thus perspired, a fair man-
And-pigeon colour vapoured out, and May
Then graciously flew in, a sloop with sail.
And at that sublime gate of icy marble
Churned water broke on marble steps, and warmer
It seemed to get from light and brawling foam,
The froth of both transparent like a poem
Of light and water, in fine unity
Of flicker-lights and water-gaiety.

And passing through that tower she passed through
A passageway, while high at the arched roof
A choir made of youthful voices sang,
Their faces white and red together crammed

To watch over the journeyings of May.
She did laugh up to them but held her way,
She still heard whispering and stories told;
And then through a long corridor of halls,
Blissfully lit; smooth walls that seemed to go
Upwards and wholly endlessly; rainbow
Of colours sieved through the transparent roof.
The floor lay full of colour-light that grooved
Through domes of glass and ice, endlessly high.
And she saw through the walls, and so her eye
Dragged ever into novel rooms, and poised
Sometimes she stood, did she not hear the voice
Of Balder sing in a far parlour hall:
Was it the cackling of light-waterfalls?
Were here the walls of water, light or ice?
Had been a palace of their own devised
By colours all alone, or were they songs
Of Balder's music that in echelons
And ranks had their halls there, where they would eat
Inside and drink of their own melody?
Sometimes she saw far in a corridor,
A white robe disappear, her calling for
Was lost then and her asking for his name.
Balder, Balder, by wall and window frame
It rustled, shivering light-waves buzzed it forth.
Once was a hall alight, just like the north
In wintertime by the blue northern lights;
There stood a single man-statue upright,
The eyes were open, finger on the mouth.
All still it was, save a gust that blew a bout
Of frigid wind that bore pine-tree laments.

Across she saw a room then radiant,
Where a young woman's statue had been raised,
There was the light of southern sun, the face
Blooming with blood, the feet standing on flowers.
A finger on the mouth and winds around her
Whirling like dreams, soft flew the blondish hair
Upwards, fell over eyes as dreamers' lair.
Onward, onward, feet treading, moving on
Over the colours, they were ice or stone,
Like jasper, mother of pearl, Norwegian
Red granite, sapphire, mirror-porphyry;
All was reflecting, and it seemed as if
Figures in there were shimmering, like leaves
Of trees in river flowing in slow rove –
For every image there lived on, once woke.
Quiet, but through the silence pushed along,
Started to drone, a noise, one hears a gong
Like that in black and Indonesian night.
Like an entire people laughing, thick, in fright.
The light was startled, briefly darkening,
But lit again, the colour-hovering
Went undisturbed from high to down below
And on and upwards once again, she floated
Towards that drone right through those colours too.
It turned heavier, though flickered also through,
Like rays of lightning, sometimes with a laughing,
Like yellow lightning when the thunder-wagon
Is pulled by Thor with thunder-load; she heard then
Gradually bright sounds like when a person
Speaks to a people, or the carillon
Is wholly chiming and a heavy storm

Of clappers is heard: like high bells of a church.
And finally she sees where in dome's arch,
A span of gates stands reined in golden bridles,
She does not see them, briefly visits, idles
Her head, then hears and wants to stay no more,
But stays and, trembling, is opening the doors.

Stillness. May too stood still. That was a hall
Of bright light, shadowless, light over all.
A row of men around a glittering
Of glass and silver, in a sweeping ring
Around a long-stretched table. One could see
No roof or walls, and there were flower wreaths
Upwards, aside, and also spun were leaves
Above, aside, with tree-light wizardry.

Far and deep, in the back sat on a rock,
Which in the distance seemed small as a block
Of ice at sea, an old and bearded man,
Who stood up, with a goblet in his hand,
He looked from far at May, echoed these words –
All rose, and stood alongside of the skirt
Of that banquet, just like the rows of reeds
Waving and bending where the river fleets.
He spoke: "A little dove came into this nest
Of cocks, if you want something, it would be best
To seek the oldest, weakest, wisest, me.
Who are you?" Finally the string of men
Silenced their bursting laughs and goblet-banging,
She said and sang this song then – just so sings
A woman in a hall, from her throat spring

The sounds into the silent air, beneath,
The listeners drink it in, walls doughtily
Resound. – And so resounded her soprano:
"Listen, listen men, your eyes now lay on
Me, listen oh king of the hall's end.
Ready the moon, ready moon's radiance,
Ready is the star-horde, ready the night,
Cold is moon-fire, cold is the winter night,
Ready is the moon-child, in this hall of kings,
Do you see the moon-child, cold as the night?"
Some shivered, one of them put to his mouth
The glowing wine, in silence all around:
"Listen, listen men, you from this residence,
Listen, oh king, to this verbal effervescence.
Gold is the sun, gold arrows of the sun,
Gold is the sun-ship, gold the sail of sun,
Golden the evening, golden the harbour mouth
From where the sun sails, at early morning hours;
Bright is the sunlight, healing the wholesome sun,
Gold is the sun-child, bright whom the sun sent down.
Do you see the sun-child, you who live here in this house?

Cool is the moon, hot is sun's radiance,
They live together in one heaven manse.
I am the moon-child, like the moon I'm cold.
I am the sun-child, hot as solar gold."

Their goblet some then slammed into mere dust, all
Of the gods were screaming, all the castle
Wavered and thundered, – at this time May went
And round the ring descended and ascended.

Where she was passing all heads followed suit,
Talking while she approached, close to her, mute;
When she had passed by them, whereas the old
Gods spoke in admiration, who were gold
Of hair still, watched her as she went and then
They hushfully returned to food and tankard.
They saw her climb upon stone rockiness,
Where high within his royal loftiness
Wodan sat low and with his beard hanging.
He had a table for himself, the ring
Of gods brought him in turn the aliments.
They now saw May approach and Wodan stand
Up. And they sat together: a dove thus sat
Once in a rack beside a horse's head.

And at the meal the gods sat at the table,
Both young and old. May looked at them, surveyed all,
She searched for Balder, but he was not there.
The table was like night sky when and where
One sees the Milky Way; the voices buzzing
Like sparkling stars at first, sometimes the bouncing
When new wine barrels rolled into the hall. A
Laughter broke loose here and that one walloped
Exuberantly round the table, first
The heads were shaking, then more still, – when herds
Of sheep are grazing that sound may be heard.
The sparkling of the drinking goblets skirted
With wine, the goblets held inside white hands
Like flowers with fine stems, and teeth like bands
Between the full and laughing lips, while eye
And cheek and hair were wettened with a shine.

The meal went on, the venison and wine
Barrels were opened, wine and blood was lying
In glass and dishes, tables flowed with it.
Wine gargled in the rummers and one pitcher
Shattered, the wine broke out like from a bomb.
Around it everybody screamed and stomped.
And slowly started swaying of the trunks
And staggering of heads, like ships that dunk
Into the waves just when the storm begins,
And grumbling humming much as when the wind
Is raging through the fish-fleet's empty cordage
That's riding in a flood on anchorage.
And thus, while all around a bright light shone,
Glory of light, in which the meal below
Seems like a tossing sea where the sun stands,
Heat blazes, water growls, then May began
And she stooped over towards the old man,
Who listened, staring still ahead, "Wodan,
Where is the fairest god, oh where is Balder?"

A tree falls down this way, as from his shoulder
His head fell forward, and his eye turned dim
While falling down, his hands were foundering
Down the table and flopped onto his knees.
He turned much older, sideways she could see
His head turn grey while yellow turned his skin.
Breathless and wide-eyed she saw shivering
And trembling all of his old body, clouds
Were passing over him, moans bellowed, loud
Oxen bellows, is what she heard in him.
Above, around a voice of hurricane

Started complaints, the air turned black, and hail
Started a table-clattering, with waddling gait
Some grasped the barrels and ox-heads, the hall
Seemed low with hazes now and with cloud-fall.
And one by one, the gods turned muter, sat
There stiff in shock, a while together yet
As they had been before, and bellowing
Like wolf howls soared now everywhere the wind.
Amidst that stumbling Wodan then arose,
An old man with grey bones, and thus he spoke:
"Gods, today all joyfulness is cursed,
It is my son, it's Balder, whom she searches."
And all the gods themselves bent down, supported
Their heads upon their arms, no one heard more than
A most lacklustre sound of mourning-moan.
And like a shepherd Wodan stood, and low
Was also bent his head, as though he a song,
An elegy, presented – on his tongue
It buzzed. The goddesses in residence
First, playing spinning, listened rigid and,
Alert like summer-flower groups, still sat:
They slowly heaved themselves, most delicate
They started whisperings, standing by each other,
Lifted their dresses up with neither laughter
Nor with bluster, in a milk-white row
Like swans migrating, went and passed below
Their lofty doors and through the portals then.
Rustling like snow they came down and descended
The thresholds, into the high windowpanes
And there heard Balder's name, and love and pain
Caused them to weep where they in bunches stood

Under the gloomy trees, and when they could
Find open flooring, they would there kneel nether.
The women-wailing rustled soft and tender
In the men's mumbling, as a water-well
Rustles in autumn forests: sad and shrill.

Just one was sad and still and that was May,
She could not weep, for she felt desolate
Inside and loneliness – for hope was lost
That had inside been playing – and the rush
Of cold blood made her body frigid then.
She sat still and just felt a quivering
Over her back, when the Asynjur[7] flight
Flew in the hall with little pigeon cries.
And she remembered now the name Idun
And looked around in search where in commune
They crouched as on the dovecote do the pigeons.
Some of his sunshine-day would surely glisten
Still in her hair and still her blood from his
Kisses would glow. But she was not amidst
The others, because she remained in bed
Where in the past young Balder came and slept
With her, and dreams like flourishing rose-bloom
Sprouted appeasing her love's bill and coo.

And then while all around the bottom droned
And thunder outside, and the gods still moaned
And mumbled, sprouted this conversing speech:
May's words like what wells up from spring-bird beaks;
But Wodan's, meanwhile causing shiverings
Of trees and leaves, the flowing of the winds.

And every time his name was dropped, the air
Was dread-struck, neither column nor god could bear
Themselves, nor any rock, nor hedge of trees.
"Balder, Balder, who's hiding him, where's he?"
"Is gone from here," Allfather[8] growled in speech.
"Does none know where, won't he come through this door?"
"No one knows that, he'll come here nevermore."
"Was he young here, happy, dancing singing songs?"
"His voice still sounds, his shadow dances where he jumped."
"When Balder came, wasn't the whole house bright?"
"Woe, woe to me, to whom he brought the light."
"Did the gods laugh then, midst blushing goddesses?"
"With him entered the halls a blissfulness."
"Was he the fairest and the gleamiest?"
"His eye most light, his voice the ringiest."
"Balder, a heaven-star and a day-flower."
"Balder, a wood-bird, Valhalla's renown."
"Balder, a fountain-well, a waterfall."
"Balder, a sun-mountain, a flower-vale."
"Balder, Balder, who knows him, where is he?"
"No one still knows," Allfather growled in speech.
"Idun, did she not love then Balder so?"
"And still, this pain she also undergoes."
"How did she wait for him, were evenings yellow?"
"On a rose bed, under a pansy alcove."
"How did he come into her arms, all tired?"
"Not like that, but crowned in rays and shod in light."
"Around him there was glory and a fragrant damp."
"Each of his hands was like a shining lamp."
"Balder, his lily skin had oily scent."
"Balder, his gorgeous blood had purple tint."

"Balder, his body like a royal throne."
"Balder, a child of kings, a Wodan's son."
"Balder, Balder, who knows him, where is he?"
"We do not know," the gods all growled in speech.

And all this time the hall with frantic whirls
Was filled in windswept vapours and with swirls
Of leaves. Meanwhile outside the water clashed
Against the hard foundations, and there splashed
In chunks the waves, they on the window drooped.
So the steam boiler howls after new scoop
Of coal and then its flame and water rage,
Just as the wind went round there and the haze
Of steam was driven forth, new ones behind.
And Wodan stood in there, from now kept quiet
His voice, the gods as well remained then silent
Like men standing towards their king inclined.

And then she said: "Now men, now you hear me,
Myself I saw him: I bring you this news."
That sun in the sad garden came and shone:
In silence climbed the fog into the crown
Of trees, clear and clearer it turned below.
An evening downpour turns the garden so
Lighter and lightest, full of diamonds
Of sunshine and of raindrops, redolent
Is every blossom, with every bush a weave
Of spider web's drip-coloured lacery.
And once more she said: "Men, now you hear me,
Myself I saw him: I bring you this news."
Once more that sounded brightening and stilled

Like balmy oil wave-mumbling, trembling still
It went forth, out, around and flew as well
Into Idun's chamber, where then she smelled
And tasted silent smoothening relief,
Arose and drank him in and she paused briefly
In a presage, what that feeling meant –
And murmured on, so murmuring she went.
She saw them standing there when she entered,
The gods and goddesses, while Wodan stern
Stood by himself – and they stood there all mingled,
Their open mouths were speaking and they twinkled,
That's what she saw, and also blushing heads
Like flowers, and eyes foretold a happiness
With glittering, up in the air large hands
Went moving, cheerfully, likewise the strands
Of satin that caressed the floor in trains.
They saw her and went like in fleet-parade
The ships, aside, but only one was staying
Deep down and at the end of the light lane.
And she, Idun, was staggering through the middle
To May and treaded close, around her middle
She gently laid an arm and her head bent
On the shoulder beside the breast: so stand
Fully sheaved two ear bundles on the land.
Out of her eyes a flickering of glances
Kept watch and then her hand began to fondle
The hair behind May, and they seemed to warble
Some thing, but that no one could understand.
The other hand held tight in it the hand
Of May like a great treasure, grabbed and pinched her,
Lifting it she kissed it and the fingers

Then, with her mouth and one by one, she counted.
Balder, Balder, it rustled and she wound the
Arms around her, as if she was Balder.
And so within the wind the long grass stirs,
Just as the words stirred her, Balder, them both,
And as the wind grabs branches, so echoed
Higher and higher, all over the crowd,
Balder, Balder, and arms folded about.
"He lives," she said, "He lives, for I saw him.
Yes, I have heard his voice, he lives and sings.
Oh gods, he sang to me a song of dreams,
A song of divine dreams, I felt not me,
Myself no more, him, him, a second him.
I scurried with him and in glistening
Infinity I ceded with his voice,
Like into cooling lakes, of sense devoid,
I was just music, and my preciousness
I felt no more, all lost but helplessness,
Melting in tones, a chord I lasted long.
I hear him so forever, have belonged
To him since then and always now, for good.
He then was silent, vanished and now too
The blood flows slower in me, deep within
Though sails the ship still of reminiscing.
He sang of you, Idun, and I have quested
Your house, your home, if maybe he there rested."

And all around were hanging happy faces
Like apples and the god-eyes' sparkling gazes,
And everyone looked all the while at May.
Idun was laughing, had herself embraced

And carried by May, laughing, both were grand.
She kissed her, and again once more, and then
Twined round her hanging like the blue flower-tendril,
Clematis flower, chalice on the slender
Swell of a vase. All noises for long quelled
While everyone there felt themselves compelled
To celebrate and all of them desired
Loud noises and loud songs: impulsive sighs
Sometimes were fleeting from constricted throats.
Till finally they heard exquisite strokes
Of fingers to harp strings, because one god
Had quietly gone out to break the lock
Of Balder's chamber, there recovering
His zither: that began its murmuring
Behind from where the multitude had piled –
And all were brightly shimmering and smiled.
A song concluded: no one looked around
But all in front of them and they bent down
The heads, this while on top of them rained sprinkles
Of tingling sounds, like little drops of drinks.
But Wodan stood up straight, and moved his hair
First back then forth over his gods down there.
When that song ended, they all spoke together
Bending towards each other, so do gather
The birds in autumn plotting their long journey.
And all were laughing and Idun was yearning
Now silently and searching the high door,
That it would open and let through her lord,
So fair returning from his voyages.
He lived, now came again, her amorous
And singing heart sang such a melody,

She, red above her neck in dreamery
And craving gave her lips to empty sky.
And around fluttered the Asynjur flight
In white with May already, asked her how
The song of Balder was, she kept her mouth
Though closed and spoke not much, but always she
Looked at Idun with love and jealousy.

A dance. And all the crowd came dancing forth where
The hall ended. Out of all their quarters
Appeared in the disturbance blonde-tressed girls.
They came out laughing, with their gowns well-furled
Around themselves, the way that some gemstones
Flicker in satin, is how these women shone
With foot and bosom from the gowns their light.
Idun led the parade, as Balder's bride,
She tiptoed on the marble with warm feet.
Then all started to dance: parades complete
Were coming forth, arms with hands interlocked
Floated ahead, behind came waves of locks
Riding along upon the air. A single
One turned the head in laughter and the tinkle
Was sounding like a Roman altar bell.
Then came the rows of gods, "Hurray" was yelled,
Resounded pounding: screamed by mighty Thor;
Behind him other gods were grey and hoarse.

Wodan stayed lonely, woeful, in despair.
When he was by himself, he still stood there
A while, weighty and sad he then sat down.
Silence and ponderings then made around

Him a dark groove, and inside that he rested.
The hall turned dark, and also all that treasure
Of banquet turned dark, dark turned too the mind
Of Wodan, in his eyes still glistened shine.
He sank in ponderings and two black ravens,
Like sextons lowering a cold corpse in the grave,
Flew in there softly and before him poised –
Still long he listened to advice and voice.

May was there still and she sat not too far
Within the dark and shone there like a star,
Attentively she looked at the old god.
Outside the masses danced, and she heard lots
Of laughter and foot-shuffling and a brisk
Conversing faintly audible, the ridge
High in the hall held haze, some wind still whizzed.
Afraid and more afraid she turned, as is
A child of an old man, herself alone.
And from her fear she stood up, ran along,
And without looking back was fleeing far,
And wandering the dark like a light star.

And she felt lonely, further fled away,
Broke free, just as a sheep that has escaped
From the angry shepherd, grazes lonely now
And can go where it wants again. Worn out
From others' happiness and her own grief,
She then walked slowly, saw not, and her teeth
She ground together, there is jealousy
In every gloomy heart midst gaiety.
And she stood still again as well, there was

The white palace behind, glittering with glass
In domes and towers, there was now inside
Once more the joyful light, the shadow-side
Was hers alone: "Oh Balder, *I* of all
Love most your young rich youth," and that consoled
Her soul, and suddenly struck high in her
A wave of pride, she shook her ample hair,
Just as a cheerful horse its tail, and ran
Faster and faster like a horse. – Again
The deep and wide and high blue opulence
Of sun and ether-fire without equivalence,
Was there, that burns itself but not devours.
The fire fights there with fire, but none surmounts.

And when she'd come far in these level grounds,
She stood for long once more and thinking, found
A great delight in her, from contemplating
Now with more certainty that her long waiting
Could not last much longer – would she soon end it
Close now to his home, would then her languid
Lips appeal for love, oh for one kiss.
She pressed close to him, and a dream appeased
Her as though he rocked her back and forth. And hither
And thither she walked herself, too, like a feather
That was lost on a pond from a swan's wing,
She almost languished there and stopped again.
And he became in her proximity
So manifest her nostrils totally
Opened themselves, as if he could there be smelled.
And then she thought of earth below, there welled
Before her eyes a flowery creation,

Primrose and violets, precipitation
Of evening dew imbued with scent came raining –
And so she smelled him, languished there and fainted.

Then slowly she was being pulled away
While she lay dreaming, as if full of flakes
A snowstorm crossed the sky. Around her reeled
The murmuring of winds, and were concealed
The legs and arms deeply in fragrant guise.
And she under her hair, which occupied
Her chest's pale flats and momentarily
It moved on wind while roaming aerily.
Then she was genuinely beautiful,
Her soul fully in her, desire could fall
No more from her, she was a flower true.
Where do you float to *now*, May you, oh you
I call my property, who long enough
Have been my dovecote, in which all the doves
Sit silent down, my thoughts, or also flock
Inside and outside and themselves may rock
Around and over you, my darling May.
Though they will likely follow you, they sway
Still tirelessly, but don't you go too far?
I hardly see you anymore, you are
A star so high, only my feeble eye
Can follow now, my lips are turning dry.
Where do you float to now, my darling May?

She had been floating long like this and raised
Herself again just like a diver straight
In water, in her hands was a bouquet

Primrose and violets, she laughed persuaded,
And certain now that Balder her awaited.
She fluttered forth but slowly she progressed
In dreams, and thought of him and first request
That she would make to him, oh just one kiss.
She felt his lips then and the gentle hiss
Of quenching on her mouth, and in her fingers
His finger vibrations, and in blonde swinging
Of her locks of hair, his breath, oh his cheek
Against hers now, and she floated oblique
Again while she proceeded as before.
Not conscious of her senses, ever more
In her were playing thoughts and arguments,
Musicians so await their audience
And try already strings of violin.
Such sounds in her, she heard not – hiding in
Herself then, not desiring to enjoy
And hear and see the tones grow gently coiled
In braids of bush with flowers prominent?
But still, while scent frolics with sentiment
In her, fingers of Balder, Balder's scent,
She sails ahead, her feet in front, and wind
Blows over her, brings alternating colours,
She first turns red, then white from feet to shoulders.
She now awakes again and see, she runs
Faster and faster, and lets her feet plunge
In twilight-fire and smoke, such is that blue.
She's cheerful now, see how aloof and soothed
She smiles out from her eyes, sees both of them,
Oh now inseparable, herself and him,
And she has both her arms around him wrapped.

She sees a golden dwelling and his steps
There cross the doorstep, and she lies inside
Over a bedstead and she feels the light
As if the red sun's entering the chamber.
See now how red her cheeks, and how the shame there
Within sets fire alight. She cannot bear
It, dreams once more. – And then again in her
Begins a song, and though she sings herself,
She cannot hear it – as from a deep dell,
That's on a shore with leaves and sun-endeared,
A source springs, its own springing it won't hear.

So sailed she on for many earthly days,
Not she or I know, how or where, a case
Of will drove her forth at her own command,
Perhaps desirous draw of a god-man.
I do not know, for all this time was I
Deep in you, May, yourself, no blink of an eye
We looked around, but felt inside of us
Deeply a warmth and softness like bird fuzz.

And when she woke up – is it not so, May? –
Then that was from a coolness: rumination
Of vapours was around and it was dimmer
From fuzzy fluid vapour, and it shimmered
Like with enormous eyes. And it was warming,
As if a fire was close, there hung no awning
Above her eyes so they could watch the stars –
But all around were clouds like conifers
In downy hedgerows and there down beneath
Like pillows of moss on which tread the feet

In springtime forest, then they are most soft.
"Not yet? Was he not there yet?" Sweet waft of
A smile showed on her cheek, unnecessary
Now to still have fear, was it not reddish,
The twilight there? Oh that should then be him.
She floated thither, but that reddish gleam
Too floated forth. That too was a great peace
To her: they went together, and beneath,
The vapour-pillows bounced, and from above
Now it turned lighter too, like a dark oven
That slowly starts to glow. Then wandered shapes
With a tall waist in light, white colour-shades
Much, much, much higher up, they scattered leaves,
Defoliating roses, they were seeds
Of light, for where they came down shot a light-
Corn harvest through the vapour, at its highest
Around May's shoulders; she was filled with glee
For he and she were so being received.

Slowly gave way all of the nebulants
Of vapour-shade, the shadow-nebulants.
They all were taking flight, and all about
She saw the fleeting of light vapour-crowd.

And slowly music started up and tinkled,
Music of little flowers and bells, and jingled
Small bell-clapper in clock-bowl's house of glass.
And every sound then shattered into shards
Both clock and clapper, as if for just one clank
Alone were they created, death for thanks.

Then music-cloudlets drifted passing by,
She saw them not, but *did* see them, describing
Stripes and rings, and how they calmly rise
In distant light, and she could realise
In full regalia their tonal riches.
And they were tender rosy, also riftless
And without burst, but busted high in rain,
Cloudburst of tone, when toneless height was gained.
They then came raining down in draperies,
Vertical rays, droplets of translucency,
Like beads on reed in an East Indian string –
Close to ears, by eyes just in the distance seen.

Both light and heavy tones fleeted away.
Then back and forth she in herself felt waver,
Like a toddler that yet wants to walk but cannot,
Her long desire, like a vigorous man
It scattered other soul-born imagery.
Was he not here yet, Balder, so thought she;
Then she could see round her but hear no more.
It seemed the earth, around there stood a chorus
Of trees: light poplars, which did not dismiss
The sunlight, but they made it, with their wisps,
Shudder and tremble. Hills climbed graciously
And flowers hung from there in quantity.
And in the distance were high-walled plateaus
From where were bending into the below
Some waterfalls making a dizzy vault.
And her desire grew so sizeable,
She bore no more of what from earth could come,
Of tears and love, and in delirium

Was feeling him in every thing: she raced
Towards a tree, and thinking him, she paced
Towards it, reached with open arms, she fell
Against it, and she kissed, a soul she felt
In him; and then into a ditch plunged she
Herself, open it lay along some trees,
Her walk enraptured, deep in struggling wet.
She loved the heaven next and measured that
Then with tremendous strides and she was drinking
Him in, caressed and ate him, and was winking
Him with her eyes and she was scurrying
Fast through him, then she felt him deep within.
She walked through meadows, and on top of hills,
She walked on mountains and through watery rills,
She walked a world through all Balder's domain,
And she was everywhere and saw the same
As him in all, not him – till she arrived
Into one vale and there himself imbibed.

And she imbibed, consumed him, *in* her eyes,
Leapt forward, grasped him and would not abide
His speaking, and instead she pressed and closed
His lips with hers, their voice was in this pose
Not heard for very long, and she sat nigh
Against him, bent herself, and passing by
His chest, her neck up high, she quenched her thirst
So, hardly breathing, with short sobbing bursts.
And finally her head fell to his side,
And on his shoulder she broke down and cried.

He was a man who, used to miracles,

Sensation-miracles, stayed equable
Therefore, and could maintain the way he sat,
While she cried out. And in himself he had
Her image soon as well, the way she wept,
And warmer he became himself and wrapped
Both of his hands around her and he held
Her so, close to him, little wept himself,
As if her woe his little sister cried
With him. She felt his wet tears, and inclined
Her head more to the side, when she saw light
Again between her tears, her face she dried.

She saw his lips again then, and to kiss
She bent over to him, and between his
He felt her lovely breath, a breath of spring,
Breezing at him and then came into him
Memories and light imagery of spring:
He was himself like spring, a carolling
Of small birds was in him like in young trees.

Once more retreating, in timidity
She sat perplexed beside him, with eyes closed,
Her hands abandoned him, then thoughts arose
Again inside his mind, like in an orchard
When children do arrive, they will for sure start
To pick the hanging apples, although nether
Fall many more, the grass seems yellow-red there.

And when she finally there in silence poured
Colourful words, the red of shame she wore,
It was to him as if the sun let suddenly

Following hush of night and make-believe
Of the pale twilight, from a swamp of clouds
Itself rise, blowing, and this blowing out
Spreads colours through the skies, over the grounds,
The water, yes all things that can't be counted.

"I am just May, I only live on Earth,
The Sun and Moon were those who gave me birth
Still small, now I am grand, for I'm beside you.
Oh make me grander, I'm still small and shy, too.
Oh let me listen here to what you'll say,
Forget all the things from my early days,
Of youth and beauty, but see all the things
Of you, a tree, and in your shadow linger.
Oh, rise above me now just like a tree,
May I then lie beneath you, and a dream
I will hear rustling wayward through your leaves.
Oh, let me be but one felicity,
A dream of you, oh, make me always rife
With you, a fruit that sunlight swelled alive.
I want to give, see, all I have to you,
Because I always did, still do, I scoop
Hundreds of things from me, that are for you.
I am just like a mine, I hurl great jewels
From my shadow and into the daylight,
Making them into mountains, the sun may cry
When he sees them, it glistens so, a brook
Streams off with tears of light to you, I broke
Myself for you, Balder, open for long.
Balder, Balder, have you not seen me going
Ever over the earth, did you not see

How all the earthly gods came offering me
All that they had, as well my merriment
In taking it all, and with it jubilant
And laughing, mirror myself in a lake,
Under the shining moon, and then to make
With it a ring around me in a chain
Of glittering and fracturing each ray –
I need no more to know that: I have you.
May I now drink your lavish kisses too,
Now that you're sitting next to me, great font
Of kisses and of play for me, I longed
For you with great desire in a night
On earth and in the heavens"– very light
As if in every kiss exquisitely
She tried to taste all of her fantasies,
And long her lips were buried inside his,
She cried again and did so without cease.
And in her voice he let himself be lulled,
Just like a bird under the sun, that also
No longer flies, but floats so aimlessly,
And feels the shining sun – and easily
His mouth allowed a kiss because her red
Melodious lips had just commanded that.

And while they there thus like a flower sat
And one beside it, that together at
The edge of woods have grown, where when wind blows
They sometimes touch each other, and the glow
Of one the other feels, with stalks that stroke
And rub along each other and yellow
Flower-honey hearts see in each other's eyes –

They sat like this while there were passing by
Many extraordinary apparitions
On heave of melody and beating rhythms.
So was that land where all that Balder thinks,
He landlord and land-god, itself would bring
Into existence and the world, and stays
Alive till by new subjects it's replaced.
For all things May before her eyes could see
Were *his* subjects, and *his* authority,
The imagery of music-spirit in him;
Inside his song that rustles on his rhythm,
But outside him the life-light twilight is,
In teeming, spinning, ghostly images.

They sat so, he made music in soft notes,
And she, not hearing, did see them approach.

A band of children fair and jumping round,
With tender white-rose glimmer, they are round
Of arms and legs, and like on chandeliers
In evening candle flames, their cheeks of cheer
Show small red flames as fruit shows on its skin.
In rows they spread, they are positioning
Next to each other: they are girls and boys.
And now seeks each their partner, and so joined
They dance then: the sweet williams can be so
Inside the woods, where sun shines, anemones
Thus grow in twos on grounds below the sea.
A fairy shows up, towards her they leap
And peep up and onto her legs they lean,
They grab her hands high, and with her they leave.

The twilight comes then and the evening green,
Transparent water-green below, there's seen
Thin dew and down around. And all grows dark
And there is no more ground, and higher, far
The night sky is becoming visible.
Moon rises, vapour teems, is it a glow
Of moss and mushroom phosphoric, and lights
The summer-lightning back and forth, do fly
The marsh fires through the sky, is it the scythe
Of moon inside her blinding light that parts
The grain, the star-crowned grain, out of her path?
The air is full of lies and hesitation,
It darkens though, and hides slowly away then
The half ring of the moon, her two sharp daggers,
Thunder goes round, while clouds float in and stagger.
It's quiet, blackness saturates the sky,
It's soaked in sultriness, empty of light,
The heart of night beats no more, it is dead,
The night-corpse is still warm, the black is red.
And violets are blooming from that black,
These two blue flower-violets, that lack
The light outside, from where?, but have within
Themselves blue light, it is by that they glint.
They spin and braid like this an ample bower,
A cradle of blue blossom, equal flowers
On either side – and then it was complete,
They faced each other as to wait and see.
And two pale beings then trod forward, close
Squeezing together, and between, below
Their arms the other's arms were laced.
The heads towards each other, face-to-face

They warm each other with their eyes and no
One there – the two of them are all alone.
The first one speaks, and it is with these words:
"I have belonged to you so long, immersed
You are in me, I don't have a remembrance
Of what's your life, and what is mine, your semblance
Am I, you're mine – if now a child were born
From us, from you and me, it would belong
To us two equally, for we combined
Deserve each other's love, I yours, you mine."
This said they disappeared immediately,
And darkness came, the violets took their leave.

And darkness around Balder too remained –
In him a heavy drone – and around May,
A flickering shone in front of her, background
Of his reflections, and they wandered round
Themselves before it, in the dark engrossed.
Raising herself she within whispers clothed,
With burning lips but also cool, those words:
"I have belonged to you so long, immersed
You are in me, I don't have a remembrance
Of what's your life, and what is mine, your semblance
Am I, you're mine – if now a child were born
From us, from you and me, it would belong
To us two equally, for we combined
Deserve each other's love, I yours, you mine."

A thunder banged and rumbled, mighty ghosts
Flew round for a brief moment, huddled close
Together they sat down, then they were startled

Away and hands fled high, they cried apart.
Balder stood high, he seemed a rock, deep blue
Was all his body, his hair black, feet too
And hands were ashen. And these words he said
Hard as a stone: "Never, never, never that,"
And blackened as a tree that's burnt he quailed.
He said it once more: never, and it came
Down as a doom upon the little May
And with her hands and feet stuck out she stayed,
Sat at his feet. Then he went wandering
Quite far from her and stood. Cold empty things
She felt, oblivious and blind she sat,
Like someone in a snowstorm frozen dead.

He stood and first he felt a deepening chill
As if he froze and turned to ice, that filled
His blue-grey hands and feet, in him a hole
Of ice, just like a berg or like a floe
Of ice that from the polar sea released
Is floating by at night, and guards the seas
In silence of the blue rays of the moon.
He shivered from his greatness and let swoon
Down his vibrations like from lofty steps,
His body, and his teeth rattled and slapped
With chats together, he like water laughed
That still falls on the winter mountains, bath
Between grim icy chunks and crusts. And he
Then laughed in gurgles, but was not happy.

He turned more silent though, for he heard choirs,
Choirs of victorious songs and lost but fiery

Resounding solos, and bright hero songs,
Bright and delicious, and appearing on
His cheeks and upwards was a bright red glow.
He stood unmoving listening to the row
Around, the wing and oar strokes of the music,
Broad strokes, as if on wings the eagles flew,
As if escaped in expiration, breaths
From broadly shouldered men, so in a quest
For space came from his chest cool sighs as well:
Like lowing of a bull, formidable
Great sounds and exhalations and his words.
He thought of May no more, forth and reverse
He strode though, stepped through heaven, in a trained
Sound-mantle he was dressed, which broadly swayed
While following his feet: a king who went
In stride through hallways of his residence.

That treading too slowed down, once more he moved
To where May sat, that thought from him removed
The dress of sound, which dropped then soundlessly
Around his feet. Over his soul a sweep
Of soft and gentle wings expanded then.
A realisation came there like a hen
Over a chick, safe on his heart in rest
It felt, as in holy of holies
The ark is standing grave and motionless.
There treading in, the floor a shakiness
Of little feet, came barefoot priestesses
With long recorders, in file with tresses
Of flower-laced and fair sweet-scented braids:
The sympathy for May, they drew away

The curtains round her, then he pictured how
She sat. He knew where she was, hunkered down
There, he again turned into the young man
As she knew him. From alabaster can,
His mouth, he poured these words out like a balm:
"Never, May, will I belong to someone,
I, Balder, someone's, see, I'm blind, can't see,
I don't see you, my child, nothing but me."
He said this and he laid as well his hands
On her shoulders, just as in the parklands
The sun thaws flowers early in the year,
She bloomed, the frigid anguish in her tears
Thawed too, when from both of her eyes they drained;
And she echoed his words, which had enchained
Her with new torment: "See, I'm blind, can't see,
I don't see you, my child, nothing but me."
And Balder spoke then like an organ playing
These words in an empty cathedral, faint
Murmur along the walls, and through the vaults –
The speaking climbs to gurgles, tonal falls
Delve open silence and the most arcane
From all corners and alcoves of the saints.
He spoke thus: "I have been like you, I'm no
Longer like that, I'm like no one, I know
My old self still, but he will soon be dead.
To see, to see, that was my prior bread
And water, and to hear and to perceive
What is around, cool colours and the heat
And respiration, that's what penetrates
All of the world, lets every being bathe
And wade through it and makes his innermost

Burn like an oven where the hell-fire glows.
And that is craving nourishment, it's callous
Desire, the opened jaw, the hand that claws
At more and more, hooks grasping fingers bent.
It changes all and it is pestilent
To all within its range, and different
It always wants what is, hates ever and
Each thing that is eternally fair and still,
Creates and bears, hating itself, it will
Not grant life to itself, but wants the grave.
Both God and people are this way, who chafe
Away at life, eroding, and they fall
To dust all one by one, a burial
Of dead desire and of withered bones.
They make new progeny, for to be gone
Is what they want, hating themselves, what is,
Wanting what comes, in rage and in sadness.

Likewise, if they can keep their sentiment
For just themselves, they are not pleased, they vent
The fury of their will and themselves too
By their creations and they build this tomb
For the most precious they are for just a trice –
Express themselves. Thus Wodan shed his light
On what he knew and felt once, he who knows
And feels, the greatest of them all, bestows
His name onto a world, now miserable,
He once must die together with his world,
Already he feels agony for both,
Joyless, a death-wolf will devour both.

Sometimes my pale old memories emerge
Still inside me and down from the breastworks
Of my palace I see the old god-world
As it was yesteryear, the flatland swirls
With dancing gods, I see large images
Of theirs to music's beat, and nebulous
In figures I still see god-apparitions.
Sometimes around me shrubs bloom, I envision
To sleep on earth then and I see the sheet
Of sea, the clouds and light that crushed to grit
Against the sky once, where is strung each star
Now, glittering within the deep blue yarn.

Sometimes I think about a woman like
When you embraced me after you arrived
Just now, kissing and wanting, without pain
Of your own feeling, love, in search of change
And the extinction of that very flame
That you had so enjoyed and that obtained
The most delightful colours in your eye.
Sometimes I feel like you still and then I
Deceived you, but I'm tranquil now and once
More true in me, feel what I always want.

Hear me now, May: there roams in all that's living,
In each body, a flame, we feel it shivering
In us one time or twice, but not much more.
It's soul as people call it, and long stories
About it, wondrous stories, they recite,
They know not much, don't nurture it, it dies
Forgotten then, abandoned and alone.

The children feel it too when they have gone
To sleep and afterwards, still long awake
And staring without thoughts ahead, for they
Can't feel an image closing in, no thing,
In them no thing's alive or pondering.
Next they feel rising up and also fall
Their life, its breathing passing through the halls
Inside their heart, beneath a high surface
Lives a new being, the broken old replaced.

This way the damsels are, when she is in
Her fuller years, shuts out long gatherings
Of man-shadows during the evening still.
Then she is sitting by the windowsill,
But she does not see through, her eyes are shut.
She does not think, life's tree is dead, but shoots
Are sprouting from the deeper life there and
She feels it wave on cool and breath of wind,
And shivers, does not bear it, her weeping eyes
Break open, then already it's passed by.

And men are so who people call the poets[9],
A young man, who forgets his mundane lowest
Life for one hour, one day, and who has heard
And listens to himself, what life is birthed
Inside himself and to the wondrous deeds
The deeper self performs, and winds replete
With sounds and words that are unheard thus far.
Maybe an hour he sits, thus feeling charmed.

That life contains an image, hear my bliss,

Now watch me rip the barrier, it is
Open, see bursting in a motley train,
Horses with bells and riders: blithe display.

That image, that is music, who can hear
Resound that wondrous gleam, will see break clear
That deepest soul, and it smashes to shreds
A prior life and with a jerk it sets
A novel stage where novel life performs:
Not understood, oh, unseen shapes and forms,
No shadow near or shine, just billowing
Air, unaccompanied soap-bubbling.

That's music, and it has no more resemblance
To any thing, and each of the strange senses
Is blind to it, it has no shape or tint,
It's similar to air through absence in
The eye and through deficiency of shine.
It is the dearest, dearest most, and minds
That wearily lived themselves with sight and taste
Of the abundant world, some drink and trace
It with their lips, want it forever on –
It gives of every thing oblivion.

Spiritual life is music: it's the soul's
Sense fully amplified, the prodigal
Eternal outpours of its sound, full baths
That boil in vapour wallowing, flawless
Gold seeds of sound, they're round, they're rounded vaults,
They're bombs of sounds, also the mows that hold
The hay and blow with light sound through the ricks.

Snowballs of music, melting out of bricks
Of ice that in own water thaws, small birds
Of music and the roaring guffaws, bursts
Of laughing men: each is a whole in all –
A people of those sounds where personal
Is each one's warble, ships in music-fleet,
Each ship is sailing on own sail and sheet,
A rain of sound relinquishing the sky,
A singing earth with one great noisy cry.

Is she then music, is then my own soul
Some thing that once outside myself did fall?

None of this is it, they are not tone,
They are not words, they are not things, no song
Presents enough the movements of the soul.
All is an image, is her image, all
Will soon or later fall as dust apart,
She stays, whatever falls and floats afar.

Therefore, who is his soul, himself's a God.
I am my soul, *I* am the only God.
There is no thing that now can heal my blindness.
My God, my soul, no image lives besides her.
When still, outside my soul exist no things,
No object, word, and none that I evinced.
I want her, and I *have*, and none but she
May be residing in this land with me.
I want no future, don't want memory,
She's always even, she's eternal, she's
Not ebb or flow, alone, for she just *is*,

She simply lives through her own genesis."

Then he stood up and May saw a blue haze
Above his head, a gleam upon his face,
A fool he stood, arms out, seeming to drink.

She knew he was not hers, started to sink
First slowly, faster then, his voice within
Her ears remained, and that was all of him.

III

It was the night
When all the clouds left for their burial.
Where I sat went a river, and there lolled
A weeping willow over me, through it
The wind wept children's tears, a soothing sweet.
Such a river in between two dykes commenced
In mountain ranges and goes by the lands
Of Germany and Holland to the sea.
The water whirred, much like a spillway's wheeze
Of water in a winter night, a tjalk[10]
Came sometimes down the stream like a dark hawk
On its two wings, with light in carmine red
Fore on its bow; that seemed a blackened head.
I heard the people's voices from the hatchway,
Meanwhile the ship sailed by, its hull in wet spray.
I felt so woeful, since the destiny
Of May I knew was tragic, I could see
Still in a mist, the long and futile quest.
The air around me moaned its sad protest,
I searched her voice but did not yet succeed.
I did hear moistened blowing through young reed,
Birch trees and little willows by the wind,
The sweet and soothing weeps, to a child akin
That walks the darkness crying without sobbing.
The branches splashed the water, with a gobbling
The water gargled in between, a fish
Alike that's swimming in the duskiness.

When I turned up my eyes, I was in thought
Where she would be? Thus wondering I sought
An answer from each cloud that I could see,
– Streaming before the skies like camel beasts
As they cross the Sahara in a trot –
Then suddenly between them I could spot
Her. Like a star first, with a twilight shine
That's lessening around, then one of, fine
And flutter-winged, the race of butterflies,
One of the children next, when much they try
To fly like birds as fowl or turkeys can,
With flapping arms without result, and then
Pale as a lily, showed my weeping May.

On pale and trembling feet she made her way
Towards me, at the stream she sat with me,
Meanwhile the trees with heavy canopy
Were whispering and they shivered like our hearts.
Though mine was boiling blood, her pain and smart
Were freezing her inside, and next to me
She didn't speak, she sat there quietly,
In humid rain on that expansive stream
Surrounded by that sombre forest dream.

By the arrival of the ruby morrow,
When from the water and the leaves the sorrow
Was fleeting and the sunlight made its home
With birds between the branches and the foam
Of waves fizzed gaily, then she let me know
What I already knew, and row by row
Said Balder's words, divine, miraculous.

Then I thought long in total quietness,
But did not understand, because my soul
Could not imagine what she'd be, when no
Longer she'd need her eyes and ears, or want
More things or something else: as can no one.

And it got warmer then, the shadow fell
Under the trees around us, and I held
Her hand. – Along the bulky dykes we strolled,
Went past the waving grass, would sometimes hold
To watch a steamboat far away come up
The stream with ships in tow, just as a tup
Is seen to go before the docile sheep.
Also awakened what had gone to sleep
Before in her and jumping down she went
And picked a flower, stood in sad content
To see it, held it to her bosom nigh.
And all the flowers tried to satisfy
Her thirst, they tripped with multicoloured glint,
Their breath into the air was redolent
And we would just continue going on.
And also down the side and by the front
That closes in the sweeping river water,
Into wide fields and meadows I have brought her,
Arriving at a silver poplar tree
We sat down there and heard the gaiety
Of leaves – and by this time the sun climbed high
And bathed the canopy in gleam and shine.

And cows were lowing when the farmers came
To milk and mow, also the window frames

And doors were creaking in a farmer's cottage.
And clouds arrived, which filled all fields with flotage
Of broken shadows interspersed with light –
The shadow came when light lost all that's bright.

Into the farmlands came the men to toil,
They filled their baskets with dark fruit of soil,
Next to each other they all made a string
Of arched men side by side and grovelling.
All these affairs we saw from far away,
The sun climbed meanwhile and the dripping shades
Of morn were turning dry and finally
They shone in gold, the lucid speech of leaves
Above we could no longer understand.

The quiet noontime: watchdogs barking when
The farmers left the field to have a bite.
They jumped and barked and pulled their leashes tight.
And mower men then lay deep in the grass,
Like white and blue shirts littering the grass.
The clouds swerved off and left the firmament,
Above the earth hot teeming in ascent.
The sun stood motionless, shone over all,
The earth was a warm sea in rise and fall.

Then I stood up and in the meadow walked
In front of her, behind then, like a dog
At times beside, at times ahead of the herd.
And every time I looked – the leafage stirred
The sunlight on her, she sat tranquilised,
Tiny and red with bare unseeing eyes,

Which flickered little beams between her tears.
I then walked on and where the meadow veers
Down to a ditch, could barely drag my feet.
The flowers growing there rocked on the beat
As they were swaying from my feet, I treaded
Above them slowly, heavy hung my head.
At foremost shrubs and bush a lady stood
Amidst the sparser bits of underwood,
Sleek willow branches were embracing her.
Indeed I knew her, she knew me, we were
Giving each other feeble smiles, for May
Had met with her before and she one day
Had tried to spare from grief her happy eyes.
She raised her hand, and such a stature high
She then maintained while pointing towards May,
She said: "She too now weeps, in this midday?"
And closer I approached her and I told
The fate of May, and all this time she'd hold
Her arm up, pointing still – such was her pain.
She herself heard and breathed now and was saying
His name as soon as I wound up my speech.
Silent, we jointly stood, her arm still reached
And pointed – over me into the heights.
We saw her both, from far and from aside,
Under a tree and finally she confided:
"Balder and May, that was a pretty dream.
Might that have been, we all could lazily
Sit back and watch the evil spirits that
Would perish; who would have inherited
The Earth? Who knows… it wasn't meant to be.
Alone again she sits – orphaned was she

Like all the women sitting on the earth,
Who once did hear his voice and saved his words
Inside their ears – I heard him too, I'm bleak,
Like under mist, the water in the creek."
A frigid springtime wind gave me the shudders,
We still stood there, turned to the child and watched her.
And then she left, the willow branches bent
Around her, but her head moved over them.

Her eyes were glowing when I turned my eyes
Towards her and I saw that she desired
Kisses and gentle fingers, her eyes turned
The heaven and the lands into a burn.
With glowing tears her eyes were being filled,
To wipe them dry she did not have the will.

It was already getting late, the meadow
Turned cooler and was covered now in shadow
And a light haziness. We went from there,
All quiet in the sundown's sunken glare.
We reached the stream again where we could see
The water sparkle and where speedily
The birds were homeward bound in sets of two.
I thought of and I yearned for my home too,
She walked with me, not far now was the town,
When slowly on our path the dark came down.
Covering the trunks first then the leaves of trees,
Coloured in red since long, and then the seas
Of darkness too washed over them, the sky
Alone kept breathing out a purple sigh.
And yellow gleaming glory from its well

Filled half the heaven in a crown of shells.
And red appearances were seen like phantoms
Painting the heaven edges that they danced on.

We saw the city gate and silhouette
Of roofs and of the tower then ahead,
Matte in the golden light of heaven's wide
Grand sea. And walls were on each of the sides
Of the gateway, through which we now went in.
Resounding echoes started there to sing,
They only came from mine, not from her feet.
The evening was inside, in yonder street
And end of the canal the twilight dwelled
Within its shady blue, the homes beheld
The night as if the lights did not yet burn.
The streets were quiet, but one could discern
In windows at the walls, betimes a woman[11] –
An old one here, a young one there, and from a
Shadowed room they watched the lighter street.
One time heard I and she the melodies
Of fiddle strings from a room at the back,
Clear carolling once from a garden shack,
A snowbird-finch, held captive in a cage.
Black figures who desired to be assuaged
Walked home like tired beasts, the linden trees
Were lining the canals all dreamily,
Swift shivers sometimes carried through tree crowns,
Whenever light wind came and tumbled down.

My house was built upon the city wall.
I opened and what mourned within its walls,

The darkness, turned to light when she passed through.
Like when in royal treasure there's a jewel,
In a dark neighbourhood it's put on loan,
Lies in a Jewish house and there its glow
And flickering makes riches from the gloom.
She was like that, the ceiling of the room
Was glimmering and the dark corners grinned.
High was the room inside that house, there cringed
Some trees down in the lowly alleyways.
The window had been opened and her face
Was reaching outside, while the roofs were here
Set up in black like coffins on high biers
Before a funeral in blackened ground.
A single little lamplight burnt around
And shadow-ghosts leapt past lit windowpanes.
A tower stood not far, on it the names
Of the twelve hours as seen on the clock's dial
Were faintly visible, and all the while
Down on the street she heard men speak together.
An odoriferous faint wind blew hither,
Like incense burning somewhere on a plate,
Distilled from dew and flower condensate,
It entered pale and passed, the watercourse
Not far, like animals, made snorts and roars.
I'd heard and seen it too, if dizzying
Were not my heart in me, these whizzes in
My ears would not be there, my eyes would not
Be nearly closed. I was not having thoughts,
New sentiments moved in me, as I sat
Deep in the darkness and my hands were wet
From fear about her body's silhouette, for there

She stood as I saw her the first time where
The willow trees were blue beyond the stream. –
We together then looked out ahead, a dream
The town before us seemed in black to dream
With all its lights out, like when languid limbs
Accompany a man towards his den,
Then dreams pay visit, dimly dreaming man.
And I then too lay down and tried to sleep
But did not sleep, and saw her, and thick sheep
Of clouds along the sky were in the window.
– And I saw her – together in a row
They climbed, in turn I saw them leave from there.
The moon shone, but I only saw the glare
Of stars and then as well their sluggish gait,
Laborious, over the house, – afraid
Of heart I stayed, she stock-still at the window.
The dark was everywhere, the silence wished though
For sounds and noise of words, its breath went heavy
From her to me, from me to her, a bevy
Of drawn-out sighs inside draped hanging vestments.
And while the silence pondered, tried to guess when
A sound would come along, while still it pondered,
Listened, guessed, just then I heard a song there
Playing, the singing of a nightingale.
It was begotten of the silence, tale
Of silence itself, as if silence spoke,
And turned unnoticed into speech that broke.

A different play of chimes the silence stirred,
Sung from a tower, by one bell at first,
By many metal others then as well.

A tree of bells while the old tower tells
A little narrative, in its young pitch.
And May looked up to it and heard the speech.
Then she came in and with the window closed,
She bolted through the room, and to and fro
She'd go for quite a while with hands together.
And she stood still, she sat and then she let her-
Self down next to me, while facing me.
Her presence made a tent embracing me
That gave to me its twilight and its shelter.
I saw two flames before me and I felt
Around me flame-lights move in whirling ways.
Her eyes were sparkling, blowing from her face
Towards me, onto me, were breaths of her
With arms held wide and coming to begird
The cheeks of me and then as well my head.
And fuller they became until I let
Their coolness quench in howl and hail my thirst,
They made deep water while themselves immersed,
Like streams that swelled and melted by the spring-
Time sending to the mountain tops its winds.
I sank in there and drowned my body deep
In ogling of the eyes and breath of sleep.

Like a soldier standing guard she lay so quiet,
The outmost outpost, listening in the night
If he can hear the enemy, he thinks
Of home, of all that's far, but hears each ring,
Suspicious and suspecting, break the night.
Then by the window passed on feather's flight,
One feather is enough for them, light elves,

And next they dwelled in front, and in themselves
They pondered long and spoke no word, one said
Something in the end, then they laughed and left.

And soon arrived a damsel, it was her sister,
She looked at her, stood by the glass and kissed her
Fingers against it, though she wiped her eyes –
June, misting round her was a lighter light. –

However, in her meanwhile beat a drum a
Roll of death – how soldiers treat their comrades
Fallen the last time before they lie
Under the earth and hidden from the light.
She felt as if cold death took its first of steps
In her, as if were dying in her lap
The children of her wishes and desire.
She lay face upwards and like that she by
Her bedstead let long locks of hair drop down.
Her bosom went with breath up-down up-down,
Her bare and pallid feet were shining in
The shadow far away and round her chin
A flame's blue breathing lightened like a lamp,
Her hands next to each other, cold and damp
And finely fingered on the woven cloth.
It all that time was as if inside her trod,
Just like a wind that roams the evening late,
Just like a child who through the old house strayed,
And then still finds some toy before he leaves,
And stands a while with it: so great a grief.

And in her it became like woods in winter,

In a horrific winter, when the wind there
In vain is blowing and the rigid twigs
And trunks that harden roughly stand like bricks
Round open patches, frozen grass, and when
The moon sheds beams like ice in the tree lane.

She shuddered and this is how I awoke:
She seemed a flower, suffering cold 'neath snow
Cover, in snow and cold it cannot sleep,
Or like a snow-white gull, a bird at sea
With its red legs. While leaning on my arm
I breathed on her and she again turned warm
As ever, for she was a sanguine rose –
And I then made my breath into what blows
Breath's glory, waves of tune and feathers' tune,
And sang a song and hushed, no gratitude
Yet given, but she sat up, me she saw,
And said, as if to perish in her voice she sought:
"You are like him, like him, in your voice as he."
She kissed me then, but really *him* kissed she
Upon my mouth, and then upon my eyes,
Although she turned her own eyes to the sky.

It then turned morn again, the dawn began
Its pouting, weeping too and mourning then
Grey tears of light while unsophisticated
And silver drops of pearl precipitated.
And finally, sun's rays appeared in all,
Which in the mornings tell of miracles,
Brand new ones, that are made of golden lines.
And we revived there in the colour-shine,

Stood up, once more between us looks we shared,
She saw me, I her, in golden locks of hair.

Then she said many sweet and little words,
I had but one wish for this morning-bird,
That she could stay there and her mouth, around
Which rising shoots of flower-words were wound.
We in the meantime stood and set our sight
On the entering golden blue and the rapid flight,
Upon and over the blue roofs, of rays.
The air was gilded by the light, ablaze
Stood on the church tower the rooster gilt,
And here and there a wind vane flirted still
Capriciously on wind, uncertain will.
And far out flew and shone the streaming fillet,
Which wafted through the meadows, where the oxen
Stood calmly and the willows stirred their lax and
Flaccid branches and their leaves like flags.
And clear lake-pools were lying there, their laughs
Resounded in the sun, an outpouring
Had left them on the ground while still the king
Of summer sun had not yet chance to dry them.
The little city lay there with mounds heightened,
Our gazes went inside and just like doves
After the flying round their cot, we saw
Slow waving, sway-waving the outer leaves
Of trees, within a greenish light, beneath
Some of the boles the grey and yellow stones,
In the canal a tow-barge slid along.
Then she asked me to see the people's town,
What works and beings could in it be found.

At the canal there was a little square,
Tree-planted, full of shadow and the care
Of thin gold sunrays, that through leaves dropped in
On elm trees, curiously eavesdropping,
In which in gold and brown the chickens glanced
On the black earth, the ruffling rooster pranced
Its feather coat and red its chanterelle.
There lay a yellow see-saw bridge, there sailed
A tow-barge by, its keel in fire-red.
The water rippled, fire colour led
In shivers to the shore upon the ripples:
On the revetment sounded wet the riffles.
Yet it was quiet still, we sat and viewed
The corner of a street, there came a few
Outside, a woman, strewing yellow grain,
The chickens cackled, flew in, unrestrained
And greedily they ate – and then a gate
Opened, a boy came out, he walked away.
All silent for a while, the sunlight climbed,
Over the gables shining bright and quiet.

There lay a workshop on that little square,
The day had waxed inside the sunny glare –
Full with a coolness and with darkened wood
It had been planked and too a ceiling put
And very old the windows seemed, where light
Of leaves shone through and through the elms outside,
A group of workers entered: grey old men.
Wood piles were there: the oak wood for its strength
And clefted northern wood of the pine tree.
The workmen took it in and tacitly

They planed and hammered on their timbering,
Industrious in the greenish shimmering.

There also was another in that place,
Dark too: the front was filled with shrouds and brace
And cordage for ship rigging, blocks of wood
And anchor chains and pulled and piled up stood
In stacks the hemp twine, and indoors there sat
The old sailmakers, who were holding head
To needle, and in front, in white, the sail.
We stood there and observed all this a while.

And we moved on, meanwhile all of the town
Came underneath the sun and toppled down
Into it like a sunlight bath, the stepped facades
Of carmine stones dried up, the nebulas
Of radiance steamed in the early morrow
And everywhere: surplus of the night's sorrow.

And we looked outwards down the passageways
And through the gates, which are like windowpanes
Inside the house: the outside-wind there flared,
The flaming light ignited, the river stared
But could not see, with pools and water dykes.
A pack mule with a heavy cart arrived,
It tugged and treaded and it clogged the gate.
A gang of sheep showed up, and in their gait
Their coats of silk-wool wagged, there rode inbound
A horseman, a farmer trotting in, a sound
Then flickered, and some boys screamed out of whack
And fought on clogs, a pub filled up, was packed.

Into neighbourhoods nearby the city wall,
The roofs were low, the doors were only small,
The streets had grass, and men were not at home.
Only the women, listening to the drone
Of fly-wings in the house, and to the steps
Of feet onto the street, and to the claps
Of neighbour doors. We heard a cranking pump
Somewhere and sometimes saw a bending trunk
Of an old lady who put out to dry
Wet linen on the hedge, meanwhile inside
The house sometimes a hungry infant cried. –
A long time we sat on the ring built wide,
The city wall, where honeysuckle climbed
Upwards with winders, awry squiggled bine
Was crawling across the wall, canals beneath
Were raucous wet, like where the Scheldt meets sea.

There too she asked me many different questions,
High climbing questions in that wagon-pleasance,
Her voice, as it rolled up the hilly steep:
We spoke for long, and meanwhile from the tip
Of the church tower we heard many hours.
The tones I heard that murmured from her mouth were
As sweet as any ever, climbed the air:
A mist to me round all horizons where
It steams with tears – a feeling of world-breadth
In me. She spoke to me about her death.

And we returned as well into the town –
The sun already from the streets backed down
And was much lower on the western rim.

The streets were quiet, boats tied at the brim
Of smooth canals were floating undisturbed there.
Around the windows, bricks were turning purpler,
The glass itself fogged blue, the curtains came
Up, climbing higher in their window frames.
The light of sun was brought then to the west,
An oriental lord, who long digressed
While riding through his town in chariot,
And now approached the palace. Face is matte,
Light yellow and light gold under the fan.
This way the sun took off incandescent
With light around, inside a palanquin
With velvet, red as wine, and carmine sheen.

And groups of women gathered then to meet
And comfort life by talking in the street,
No easy life, and greybeards took the lead
Enjoying the late life, they sat at ease
On pavements close to home, and watched in peace
Over their glasses people and all things.
A scaffold by a house still lingering,
From there the masons climbed down in a row.
A young man with blonde hair did not yet go
Down with them but there on the top he stood.
As one can see a heron in the woods
Stand in a treetop – and around he gazed
At the yellow-red and black evening of day,
Smiling into the night, humming a song
He went descending, unaware, along.

The night returned, though lights did not yet burn.

The streets turned quiet, but one could discern
In windows at the walls, betimes a woman –
An old one here, a young one there, and from a
Dark and shadowed room they watched the street.
One time heard I and she the melodies
Of fiddle strings from near a home's back door.
Clear carolling once from a corridor,
A snowbird-finch, held captive in a cage.
Black man-shadows that longed to be assuaged
Came home like tired beasts, the linden trees
Were lining the canals all sleepily,
Swift shivers carried over the canals,
When on the water wind laid down itself.

When then the night came following the day,
Black-handed and black-born, that's a disgrace
Of earth, inside my house we scaled the flights.
At home we sat together in the night.
And did not sleep and did not dream, we sang
The songs of sleep and death. The cheeks those can
Turn paler, and they smother passionate
A voice inside one's throat. Pale yellow sat
There May in front of me, her mouth agape,
The sounds would come in masses to escape,
Like men and women at a funeral
Caught in a day of grief when out they walked.

And thus she sang sometimes alone and then we
Both, like sombre saddened choirs. Of many
A thing she ever had beheld, the name
Repented shivered from her tongue again

In plaintive song, monotonous long grief,
A happy note just once or twice, when she
Flared up her eyes, a beacon seemed her head,
And when ahead of her the arms she stretched.
But then she sank back in benightedness
With both her arms and with the lightlessness
Around her head, like buzzing of the bees
Her song then buzzed, just like her silent weeps.
For hours on end then, we, preoccupied
In silence, hushed, meanwhile around us quiet
Was shivering, flickering of the lightlessness
That shudders in the eyes, like sightlessness.
Outside we heard no thing, just like a grave
My room seemed then, that's lying far away
From all the people's treading in the lap
Of searing wasteland, and as hours elapsed,
The red of morn could see it after eve –
Likewise, the eyes of both of us could see.
And thus came at long last the final day,
Ferocious laughter on this pyre day,
Of flames around the wretched burning wood.
In twilight still and when around us stood
The frigid morning light, she came to me
And kneeled, down at my knees and heavy she
Laid down on me her head and when I kissed –
And I held my hand on her locks – a kiss
On the blonde hair, that time she just kept quiet,
Initially without cry, like a child,
But I could feel her breath in shudders, shakes
And burning from her mouth, and then like flakes
Of snow so slowly, drifted heavy tears

Down from her cheeks. – As sunlight disappears
From evenings, from her body also drained
Much light now – like an altar she remained,
Where fire only feebly burns in the dark
Of night-time, where just glows in wait one spark.

And when she stood up, next to her stood I –
She still was sparkling at me from her eyes
And from her hair – once more she laid her head
Close next to mine, but now her eyes turned dead
Again, as they behind her tears had glazed,
The arms around me, just like moon's embrace,
Whose arms are always light and full of grace.
And so she also brought her mournful face
Close next to mine and stood for very long,
Her eyes in mine, my perished heart succumbed.
And then she left, her mouth would speak no more,
And she walked backwards and when in the door,
Her eyes continuously on me, she stayed.
And then she left and I was without May.

And drunk she came into the light, outside,
She was intoxicated by the night,
And mutiny against dark by morn that chooses
Its chieftain: he's the sun, and then it loses
Itself for him, his shine. And it already
Falls in and blends and dies there after deadly
Dichotomy with dark, which also died:
He, proud and gay, remains and's shining bright.

She sad and lonely came into that day.

The trees within their foliage portrayed
The morning winds, there on the bastion
The youthful birds sat or like from a gun
They flew from branches high above the wall.
The bells then rang an early morning call,
Dreary and dreamily she glided forth,
Out of the gates, past levees and the board
That's wrestling with the water of its stream.
She thought of me and how I now might be
Without her, whether there'd be one such love
For me to shortly find, whom as much love
I'd give as I'd already felt for her.
She thought of death then, looked for what occurred
To her dead in the grass, but there was neither
Death nor sorrow: springtime shoots new life
In every flower and in every herb,
It's full of power, shine, straight out of earth. –
And so her final day was turning glum.

But smiling then commenced her father, sun,
A newer shine and most immaculate he
Around it wrapped a light immediately,
Collecting from his kisses, what's conferred
Habitually just on the best of earth,
Clear lakes midst mountains, mountain full of snow
Where it's impossible for us to go
And see, perhaps one man per century.
She saw that, felt first wish, reality
Then, to be just like that herself inside,
As cool as gold, and cool as a small child
Still living between happiness and grief.

And she became like that, the rich sun weaving
One veil after the other round her eyes.
Then one by one were vanishing the horizons,
High-rising bluer skies and very close
The trees and foliage had gilded clothes.
All was one colour, all identical,
Within herself she felt as plentiful
As he who is forever lone and can
No longer lose or squander other than
Only *his* life and what inside him lives.
Beneath this golden archway, this God's gift
She was already marching on, it slid
With her, most golden she herself in it,
The golden hair round her a sheaf of wheat,
From it the ears hang down, rally round it.

She came then – oh I do know where it was,
It was in youngest most pristine of grass
Between four oaks that from the blood of spring
Had still their red leaves red, could by no thing
Be harmed, but by the light of dawn be kissed,
Trembling, then by each other they were eased.
That chapel then was filled up with her glow,
The leaves gleamed brilliantly on their below,
Between the green of leaves were blue the heavens,
Unmoving leaves, the wind was mute and deafened.

That was the earth's holy of holies,
She stood there: all was straight and angleless,
Her neck, her knee, now all without distress.
That final day she stood thus, prettiest

That morning, the most gilded one on earth.
She thought still much, but in her calm occurred
No thing like an avowal: one thing she felt,
'T kept her red blood and the fair body chilled.

Like a ship that on summer morning sails
Into wide open sea, with heavy sails,
But lightly heaving on the flood of waves,
The head is clean, the foot's within the spray:
So floats the barque that comes a summer's morn,
In sight and out of dark, from night withdrawn,
The sun's rays on the mast themselves adorn
With golden streamers, ripples near the fore
Around the bow as well now streaming gold –

Like early on a summer morn when goes
A child into the park and to and fro,
With sunlight laden, over smoothened road,
Wading through light, filled with a sunny glow.
What tingles in her heart she does not know –

Like summer red a flower, poppy, which
Is standing calm full-red in bloom, amidst
A roar of sun-fire as that falls and breaks
The ground, scorching the grass it suffocates:
Yet its delight remains as great: it lets
In wind wave, hang in sun, its vane of red –

Like that she stood in greatest stillest glee,
Uncomprehended, in the ardency
Of God the Father, held the head up high,

And still her arms, and nothing on her mind.

Her head began a delicate incline
When filled became the fullest hour, declined
Her lashes dreamily, and very slow.
She tenderly turned paler, ebb and flow
Of pale and red passed over tired hands.
A golden haze evaded; it banished thence,
With light-walled bastions, and was carrying
All not completely clean and capturing
Live elves so that that place of holiness
Remained hers only, like a bowl that is
A lucid pond in which floats none at all,
But one swan and even she unmovable.

And all around, like on a lake, the meadows
Were sprinkled bright with sparks and without shadows,
Just as one finds on the great meres of sea,
The hour the sun of midday takes its seat.

Like a great tower that the sun enfolds,
Which block on blocks of mason-stones uphold,
Fine granite's higher up, there shines the sun,
Evening arrives, and from the horizon come
The rays, and it is getting darker, older
And from its feet up to the higher shoulder
It's filled with shadows and the older age –

Like the oak that on mountains under rage
Of flames, there where it is on fire, has bent,
By lightning struck, and burns the smallest branch:

It seemed a house of fire on that crown.
A dark rain fell, extinguished and bent down
The trunk that is all charred and blackening,
Still on some twigs dance tiny flaming things –

Like summer red that poppy flower, when
Wrinkling its red it withers while it bends
Its shank and sinks its tender stem down slowly –
Just so bent May as well her head down slowly
And pale and paler turned those cheeks of hers,
And the desire too turned weak and weaker
That burns inside the eyes of mortal man.
And far and further back that circle went,
The woolly band of fire, cavaliers
Alike that ride out wide to mutineers
On the attack: they cause a widespread still.

Within herself she felt one last thing: will,
The very last of will of those who die, and
The will for being dead, causing mankind
To halt its wanderings, and leads the way
Into the ground, to where the body stays.
She dizzied and was in that dizziness
As light as when a feather disconnects
From a dove's wing: she sank and did not fall:
Like that falls in the stream from reed a haulm.

Like a child who among the living was,
Like summer red a flower in the grass,
Red poppy that now on the bottom lies.
Just so she lay and then the last sunlight

Shone onto her, made her a little red
And final gold – and then they both were dead.

The moon came up when she had died, and was
A cover over earth, and from the grass
Lifted the dead-cool body she reclaimed.
What was remaining still of her warm name?
Surrounded thus by blueish light, her face
All grey from grief and with a robe in greys
Of grief and sadness trailing her, she went
High over meadows and towards me then.
I saw her when she stood outside the town,
The child inside her arms, and I sat down
No longer, went to her, up with her, nigh
To her, so I could see the child, raised high.
And I, when we arrived at the great stream,
Came down again, and she laid at its rim
The child now pale and while I wept and wept,
My eyes and head broke down, she left and swept
Her light full on the world down from the sky.
I knew what I would do and her desire,
And in a boat I then went down the stream,
In buzzing water through low land – the sea
Met with its water there, and I climbed out.
Along the beach I went with her, no loud
Noises were made, but still we had been heard.
For from the hinterland the elves emerged
And from the air the heaven nebulants,
And from the sea the Tritons, they commenced
Closely behind me then to sing their song.
And the twelve hours who already long

Were waiting for her and their grievous charge:
They had a bier, the face upwards, they marched
On ever further, carried it and kept her
Up. I in front, I, who'd been her good shepherd
And there were always more and more behind:
They came out from the dunes time after time
Descending, sliding, out from all the waves
Were sticking Tritons, body buried, they
Were singing singing the dead corpse's keen.
And when we came to that shore of the sea
We stopped, where she originally beached.
Meanwhile the dunes filled up, the water seethed
In its eternal flames, and it stood full
As well, and light-shapes were in numbers too,
Like fumes alight, they floated high above.
The gnomes started to play their drums first off,
And then the elves their cymbals, Tritons then,
We all together then, narrations and
Narrations long of song and misery.
Aware of their responsibility
The hours then set her down, let me alone
With her and then they all left in a row,
And they looked on together with the others.
I dug a grave where waves would come to cover
The sand, it was in there I laid her down,
And sand on top of that: the waves come round
And down again with laughter or dismay –
And there lies, buried deep, my little May.

Synopsis

Book I - The girl May is born from the Sun and the Moon. She arrives on the shores of Holland and travels through the flowery dunescapes. The sea and all its magical creatures celebrate May's arrival, but at the same time, they mourn her sister April's death. Everywhere May sets foot, springtime comes to life in all its wonder and beauty. May eventually meets a stream lady, who tells May of the coming and going of the seasons. May also meets the poet, but soon she leaves him, for new paths are inviting her.

Book II - The poet waits in vain for May, while she has moved on and travelled far. She has heard a mesmerising voice in the distance and longs for more of it. Then the young god Balder appears. He sings of how he was once all-powerful, until one day he woke up blind and in loneliness. But he leaves May behind. She is now desperately in love and rises through a magical cloud-world in search of him. She ends up in Valhalla with the supreme god Wodan and Balder's bride Idun. They are delighted to hear that Balder is alive, but they don't know where he is. May runs off and is then pulled into a world of music that is Balder's soul. Balder himself approaches her. He tells her that he wants to be eternal and therefore must remain with his soul only.

Book III – May, disillusioned, has sunk back to Earth. There she reunites with the poet. He shows her the bustle of his town, but that cannot console her. May spends her final days with the poet. While her sister June arrives and May withers, the city life continues undisturbed until finally, and inevitably, the poet is left without May.

Herman Gorter (1864-1927)

Gorter was born in Wormerveer, a rural town in the north-western Netherlands. His father, a pastor, died when he was six years old. Gorter studied classical languages in Amsterdam and became a teacher at a high school.

In 1889, after three years of work on his epic poem *May* (in Dutch: Mei), Gorter finally could proclaim "the thing is done." *May* was published in the contemporary periodical *The New Guide* (De Nieuwe Gids). It was a retrospect of Gorter's youth, borrowing both form and theme from John Keats' *Endymion* (1818), yet tracing its way through a wide range of impressions: of nature, music, love, the search for the divine, disillusion, transience, and melancholic reflection. Spontaneous and full of vibrant imagery, *May* quickly became a landmark of the 1880s literary movement in The Netherlands, the so-called 'Eightiers' (Tachtigers), which attempted to reclaim aesthetics for art.

In 1890, the even more innovative *Verses* (Verzen) were published, in which Gorter digs further and tries to let his spiritual and sensual emotions express themselves. Always in search of the ultimate form of poetry, Gorter would gradually distance himself from the individualistic 'Eightiers' movement. He became increasingly politically engaged and turned to expressing his Marxist ideals through his work, for example in the epic poem *Pan* (1916) and *Lyrics* (Liedjes, 1930). Gorter however never gave up his identity as a poet. Love remained a key theme in his work until his death.

Acknowledgments

This translation would not be in your hands without the support of a number of people. Hein Ouwersloot introduced me to the beauty of *May*. This translation is an ode to his spirit. My friend Michan Biesbroek, for about a decade or so, has been suggesting translating the work into English, for still no English translation was available. In the meantime, a new spring had arrived in my life: my twin daughters. Thus, I decided to finally take on the challenge. My wife Maria Kozlovskaya ensured I could distract myself for the many hours needed. Competent redaction has then been performed by Myrte Leffring, Vicky Francken and Anne Walter. Lloyd Haft contributed many suggestions to this revised edition. Their expert eye has been indispensable and ensured a much better read. Thank you.

The translator

Notes to the text

1. *May*'s famous opening line gently refers to the iconic first words of John Keats' *Endymion*: *A thing of beauty is a joy for ever*.
2. *Cynthia* refers to the moon goddess, also known as Selene.
3. *Zephyr* is the personified west wind from Greek mythology, a gentle breeze.
4. *Titania* is the Shakespearean fairy queen; *Oberon* is her husband.
5. A reference to similar lines sung by Cynthia in John Keats' *Endymion*: *There is not one, / No, no, not one / But thee*. It contrasts Balder's looking inward with Cynthia's love for the mortal Endymion, and may thus be seen as a presage to Balder's later rejection of May.
6. *Valkyries* or Walküres are mythical female figures who decided who would live and who would die in battle.
7. The *Asynjur* are the female members of the Æsir, the principal pantheon in Norse mythology.
8. *Allfather* refers to Wodan (also known as Odin), the supreme god in Norse mythology.
9. Gorter may well be describing his own soul-searching here.
10. *Tjalk* is a traditional Dutch boat for shallow water with two keels, one mounted on either side of the hull.
11. Interestingly, this line occurs identically further in the text.

Also available from Arimei Books

Herman Gorter: Selected Poems

Translated by Lloyd Haft

Volume 2 of *The Essential Gorter*

This is the most extensive selection in English of poems by one of the all-time great Dutch poets, Herman Gorter (1864-1927). A companion volume to M. Kruijff's translation of the epic *May*, this book welcomes the reader to the rich spectrum of Gorter's lyric verse.

The selection traces the stages of Gorter's career as a poet. It opens with 22 poems from his introvertive 'sensitivist' *Verses* (Verzen, 1890) which have been called the beginning of modern Dutch poetry. These are followed by poems from later collections in which Gorter was transitioning to a less self- and more world-focused perspective. In the subsequent passages from the long epic *Pan* (1912/1916), he has clearly become a 'socialist' poet, albeit in a unique visionary sense. He is now pursuing a theme which will obsess him for the rest of his life: how to address the object of his love as both an individual woman and an incarnate summation of all humanity.

The rest of the book comprises the first publication in English of Gorter's little-known last work *Lyrics* (Liedjes, 1930). Haft's judicious abridgment preserves the structure, erotic themes, and lyric high points of this outstanding sequence which originally occupied three volumes.

In Haft's version, Gorter sounds the way he should sound: musical and sensitive, at times groping, at other times jubilant, always sure of himself and amazing... For readers of English it will be a feast to be able to make his acquaintance via this translation. – Piet Gerbrandy, winner of the Herman Gorter Prize for poetry.

Made in the USA
Monee, IL
08 July 2026

56552851R00098